Letters to Our Grandchildren

Biblical Lessons from Grandfathers to their Grandchildren

Edited by Doy Moyer

Copyright © 2017 by Doy Moyer
All rights reserved.
Moyer Press, Birmingham, AL
www.moyerpress.com

Version 1.1, November, 2020

Front cover photograph by Audrey Moyer

ISBN-13: 978-1981748716
ISBN-10: 1981748717

Contents

Introduction 5

1. Learning to Learn (*Mike Wilson*) 9

2. Love God with All Your Heart (*Steve Klein*) …...............................19

3. Love Your Neighbor As Yourself (*Wilson Adams*) 29

4. Love Your Enemies (*C. G. "Colly" Caldwell*) 43

5. Stay True to the Word (*David Carrozza*) ....…...................53

6. Be Different (*David Posey*) …...63

7. Stand Firm (*Gary Kerr*) …..75

8. Learn to be Content (*Jon Quinn*) 87

9. Learn to Grow (*Leon Mauldin*) …..............................…............99

10. Learn to Forgive (*Jim Deason*) …...109

11. Control Your Emotions (*Warren E. Berkley*) …......…..................121

12. Respect Mom and Dad (*Bill Robinson*) …...….........................131

13. Develop Your Mind for God (*Doy Moyer*) 139

For our children and grandchildren

For parents and grandparents who are devoted to training up their children in the discipline and instruction of the Lord

For adopted children and the parents who have adopted them

For *Sacred Selections*
Thank you, David and Dana Carrozza, for your unwavering devotion to the children in need

"Grandchildren are the crown of old men, and the glory of sons is their fathers" (Prov 17:6).

"I have no greater joy than to hear that my children are walking in the truth" (3 John 4).

Introduction: Letters to Our Grandchildren

"Grandchildren are the crown of old men, and the glory of sons is their fathers" (Prov 17:6).

How true is this statement! "There is nothing like grandchildren." I remember being told this many times before my own grandchildren came along. I had no reason to doubt it, but it became such an important reality to me when I became a grandfather indeed. It's impossible to express fully the love that we feel for our own children, and then their children. We want them to be blessed, to do better than we have done. We desire only their good, and we want them to be a blessing to others.

My own children were blessed with grandparents who care deeply for their spiritual well-being. This has burned into our minds the need to be such grandparents to our grandchildren. My father-in-law, known as "Grandfather" to my children, would always give the *grandfatherly talk* to his children and grandchildren whenever we were together, and my children remember these talks well. In fact, they and their cousins would insist on these talks. The influence that both Grandfather and Grandmother have had on their grandchildren—my children—is profound and beyond words to express. Grandfather's expectations were always high. His children would serve the Lord! His grandchildren will always stay faithful to God! That's just the way it is.

And so it is. We have the same desires and expectations. Yet, as a grandfather myself (Papa), I have wanted to leave behind something that serves as a reminder to my grandchildren about how much I and their Marmee love them, and how much we desire for them to serve God well after we are gone. We entertain no thought of failure in this. The expectations must remain high. We know that our own examples and relationship with them is foremost in this.

As a small part of leaving behind a legacy, I thought of such a book as this. Let me speak about the other authors of this material. I began to think of how valuable it would be to hear from other grandfathers whom I know feel the same way toward their grandchildren as I do toward mine. Now, having received the input of twelve other grandfathers, I am convinced that this is a great blessing to get the wisdom and knowledge of such fine men who devote themselves to God and His word! They have also devoted themselves to their families, and what they all have to say is immensely powerful and valuable. Would that all of us read their words! Herein you will find some of the most important principles and topics that we could think to cover written by men who have the wisdom and experience of faithful grandfathers who earnestly desire to see the following generations become blessings to others by serving the Lord faithfully. Of course, there are many more preaching and teaching the same messages, and we pray that grandparents will see what a magnificent blessing it is to influence grandchildren for the Lord.

Part of the key to understanding this effort is to realize that we are all children and grandchildren ourselves. What is written in this book, though addressed personally from our hearts to our grandchildren, should be read as applicable to all of us. We are reading the hearts of wise men of God, but we are also seeing the practical applications from Scripture that affect every reader no matter how young or old. As such, the work may be suitable for classes, personal devotion, and certainly for family studies.

When Moses taught the new generation of Israel, just before they entered the Land, we read this:

"Now this is the commandment, the statutes and the judgments which the Lord your God has commanded me to teach you, that you might do them in the land where you are going over to possess it, so that you and your son and your grandson might fear the Lord your God, to keep all His statutes and His commandments which I command you, all the days of your life, and that your days may be prolonged." (Deut 6:1-2, NASU).

"That you and your son and your grandson might fear the Lord your God" should stand out. Grandparents have a responsibility, and a grand privilege, to help teach their grandchildren the ways and the gospel of the grace of God. While we like to "spoil" them a bit and have great fun with them, grandparents need to keep their eyes focused on the goal of pleasing God. Typically, they will be one of the most significant influences their grandchildren will experience. For myself, and no doubt all grandparents who would love the Lord, the most important legacy to leave is that of children and grandchildren who fear the Lord (cf. Eph 6:4). No material legacy can match the spiritual legacy of those who are faithful to God.

When you purchase a book, you are purchasing a product. On the publishing end of it, while we could keep royalties as personal income, we are choosing *Sacred Selections* as our personal recipient for the purpose of helping in adoptions for Christians. This is nothing to boast of on our part; we just want people to know what's happening. Those who are familiar with *Sacred Selections* know the great work that they have accomplished and continue to do so. David and Dana Carrozza have inspired many to adopt, and they have been able to spread the spirit of adoption into the hearts of so many Christians. It's about the children, and as this work is dedicated to teaching children (of all ages from infant to the aged), we wanted children to benefit. For the record, *Sacred Selections* is entirely individually funded. It works because committed individuals put forth the effort across the world to make it work. This book is also the effort of individuals who want to see adoption succeed. In all of this, we pray that God be glorified.

"I have no greater joy than to hear that my children are walking in the truth" (3 John 4).

Doy Moyer
Dec. 2017

1. Learning to Learn

Mike Wilson

Dear Kate, Landon, Jack, Eli, Anna, and Wilson,

I'm writing this letter while you're still young, but one day I hope you read it when you are old enough to fully understand it. I might even be gone by then. If so, it will be a great blessing to be dead but still speaking to you (Heb 11:4). I hope you will remember how much I love you, because this comes from my heart to yours.

From the time each of you showed the first signs of personality, I could tell that you were full of curiosity! I could see it in your eyes, in your mischief, and in your incessant demands: *"Tell me a story about…"*; *"Why…?"*; *"Let me see it…!"*; *"Teach me how to…."* You wanted to know about *everything,* and there was a big world of colors, objects, and ideas just waiting to be discovered. Even when you were very small, you were like little sponges, soaking it all in, whether at the zoo, at a children's museum, at the park, or in the pages of a book. I've always been amazed at how fast you learned new things.

Light a Fire

As your Grandpa, one thing I want to pass on to you is a lifelong desire to keep on learning. Never stop! Your success in life and in eternity with God depends on your personal and spiritual development. Light a fire, and don't let anyone squelch your enthusiasm for learning new things.

I believe learning should be fun. We're all different. When parents are told to "train up a child in the way he should go," teaching children to be godly is certainly a big part of that (Prov 22:6). However, the gist of the idea is to instruct a child "in his own way"—presumably in keeping with his or her natural interests, personality, and disposition. Learning will come more naturally if you *enjoy* doing it. Therefore, I would strongly encourage you to develop worthwhile pursuits where you have a genuine interest. Chase your dreams. The writer of Ecclesiastes, in developing our purpose in life, says, "Walk in the ways of your heart and the sight of your eyes. But know that for all these things God will bring you into judgment" (Eccl 11:9). A wise man once remarked, "If you do what you're really interested in, you'll never work another day in your life."

Set High Expectations

Aim high in your learning curve. Don't ever settle for mediocrity. Since God's people are supposed to be "the salt of the earth" and "the light of the world" (Mt. 5:13-16), aspiring to be "average" doesn't cut it. Don't try to blend in with the crowd. Rise above the crowd. Always strive for excellence. An *outstanding* effort is one that *stands out* from that of everyone else. Working harder, longer, and with godly wisdom will put you ahead of those who are infatuated with lesser goals. God will reward you and give you good success, if you entrust your life's work to his glory. You have all made me so proud to be your "Papa Mike." I hope you will make the achievement of excellence a lifelong pursuit. The only way to experience the most abundant fruit of your labor is to develop a strong motivation to continue learning. You have to exude a burning desire to continue working hard to master a skill and become totally proficient in it, even when others quit. This *staying power* is 99% of the key to your success.

Focus on Spiritual Development

We learn many things in life, but I would strongly urge you to prioritize the things of God. Why emphasize *spiritual* things?

1. Because they are central to your purpose in life. When Jesus was still a boy, he "increased in wisdom and in stature and in favor with God and man" (Luke 2:52) – i.e. he grew physically, spiritually, and socially. The spiritual component—"favor with God"—is by far the most important part of your development. After ruling out all the alternatives, the wise man concludes the book of Ecclesiastes on this note: "The end of the matter; all has been heard. Fear God and keep his commandments, for this is the whole duty of man. For God will bring every deed into judgment, with every secret thing, whether good or evil" (Eccl 12:13-14).

2. Because they are more important than physical development or sports. I've always enjoyed a bit of exercise or a good sports contest, but our physical bodies will deteriorate. No one stays in peak physical condition for very long. The apostle Paul writes, "For while bodily training is of some value, godliness is of value in every way, as it holds promise for the present life and also for the life to come" (1 Tim 4:8).

3. Because they are more important than academics. The universities are full of very intelligent people, but many of them are fools when it comes to life's greatest issues. Academic training has its place, but the attainment of godly wisdom will cause you to advance where it really counts. "The fear of the LORD is the beginning of wisdom, and the knowledge of the Holy One is insight" (Prov 9:10). "I have more understanding than all my teachers, for your testimonies are my meditation" (Psa 119:99).

4. Because they are more important than money. Money is a necessary tool to function in this world, but it should never be idolized or worshiped as an ultimate end. Jesus says, "For what will it profit a man if he gains the whole world and forfeits his life? Or what shall a man give in return for his life?" (Matt 16:26).

Jesus on Learning

Our Lord himself believed in the importance of learning. He says, "It is written in the Prophets, 'And they will all be taught by God.' Everyone who has heard and learned from the Father comes to me" (John 6:45). When Jewish leaders tried to confront him in Jerusalem, an interesting exchange occurs: "The Jews therefore marveled, saying, 'How is it that this man has learning, when he has never studied?' So Jesus answered them, 'My teaching is not mine, but his who sent me. If anyone's will is to do God's will, he will know whether the teaching is from God or whether I am speaking on my own authority'" (John 7:15-17).

Jesus had not gone to rabbinical school, so they perceived him as "uneducated," at least through the proper channels. However, Jesus responds that those who hunger for truth will know it when they see (or hear) it. It is much more important to develop a burning desire to be self-taught than to go through a formal education and learn nothing. This is especially true when we are weighing the answers to spiritual questions. If we do not develop a mindset to receive the truth with humility and hunger, then we are prone to believe a lie, with disastrous consequences. Unfortunately, a proper disposition to genuinely learn the Word of God is rare, and the masses allow themselves to be brainwashed. "The god of this world has blinded the minds of the unbelievers, to keep them from seeing the light of the gospel of the glory of Christ" (2 Cor 4:4).

Develop a Love Affair with the Bible

Deuteronomy 6:4-9 contains the formula for success in learning spiritual things. There is a three-step process:

1. Love God first. "Hear, O Israel: The LORD our God, the LORD is one. You shall love the LORD your God with all your heart and with all your soul and with all your might" (Deut 6:4-5). Only when we love God with every fiber of our being – first and foremost – can we position ourselves in the right place to receive his truth.

2. Get into the Bible, and let the Bible get into you. "And these words that I command you today shall be on your heart" (Deut 6:6). Read the text. Meditate on it (Psa 1:1-2). A wise elder used to say that young people need to "wear out the seat of their pants studying the text." I would add that it takes hard work until we begin understanding the interconnections – and then it starts becoming fun. God's Word is our spiritual mirror (Jas 1:22-25) and night vision goggles (Psa 119:105). In it, we see life, including ourselves, through God's eyes.

3. Get the Bible out of you, and into the hearts of your loved ones. "You shall teach them diligently to your children, and shall talk of them when you sit in your house, and when you walk by the way, and when you lie down, and when you rise. You shall bind them as a sign on your hand, and they shall be as frontlets between your eyes. You shall write them on the doorposts of your house and on your gates" (Deut 6:7-9).

First, notice that God's Word should be taught (and learned) "diligently"—not in a haphazard, hit-and-miss way. The learning process should be intense and strategic. Second, notice how often should be the exposure to the Bible: "when you sit… when you walk… when you lie down… when you rise" – i.e. at any opportune moment, all the time. Third, "bind them as a sign on your hand" and forehead – i.e. not something to be treated as minor or incidental, but rather something you essentially wear, close to the vital organs. Finally, "write them on the doorposts… and on your gates." The holy scripture is so important that you post it as a visual aid, so that it is the last thing you see as you leave home, and the first thing you see when you return.

Transmitted with Passion

If your parents do their job well, and I believe they take their responsibility very seriously, they will raise you "in the nurture and admonition of the Lord" (Eph 6:4). Read Proverbs 2:1-12; 3:1-12; and 4:1-13, and see how passionate Solomon is about his son learning what he has to say. He is saying, in essence, "Listen up! This is really important! You need to pay special attention to what I have to say, because it will have a huge impact on your future well-being." It may sound like badgering, but I hope you come to know that it takes a great deal of love to tell someone what he or she needs to hear, because an eternal destiny is at stake. Please let your parents do their job, and receive the message in the spirit in which it is intended. Of course, the same holds true for this letter from your Grandpa.

Tie the Commands of God to the Greatness of God

Transmission of the faith from one generation to the next is more important than transmitting a physical genetic code. Paul spoke to Timothy about the "faith that dwelt first in your grandmother Lois and your mother Eunice and now I am sure, dwells in you as well" (2 Tim 1:6). It marks a big step in your development when you receive what is passed on and decide to personally "own" it – i.e. when it really becomes part of your personal spiritual DNA.

Psalm 78:5-7 says, *"He established a testimony in Jacob and appointed a law in Israel, which he commanded our fathers to teach to their children, that the next generation might know them, the children yet unborn, and arise and tell them to their children, so that they should set their hope in God and not forget the works of God, but keep his commandments."* Notice the connection between the "works" of God and the "commandments" of God. If there is one thing I would counsel parents to bequeath to their children, it would be to tie the Word of God to the greatness of the God who revealed his will to us. In order for you to appreciate how important the truth of God is, you must realize how big God is, and what great things he has done for us. If your view is fragmented, and you see the commandments as nothing but disconnected "dos" and "don'ts," without plugging into the greatness of God and his efforts down through the ages to reach lost men and women, then you will never reach your full spiritual potential. The ability to genuinely learn the will of God always starts with our view of God himself.

Dive into the Stories of Bible Heroes

Another factor that will make learning God's Word relevant, and help to write God's new covenant on your heart, is to read the rich treasure trove of stories embedded in the sacred text. Little children love to hear stories of David and Goliath, Daniel in the lion's den, or Jesus feeding the five thousand. God is the supreme Storyteller, because his Word is full of great epics of past heroes. These episodes build our faith, they build our character, they build our respect for God, and they give us a moral compass.

There are three things about Bible adventure stories that I want you to remember. First, the stories are there to help us learn better what God wants us to know. God knows that we remember important principles when they are communicated in a real-life situation. These were real people who had problems, just like we do, yet God worked powerfully through them. Second, the stories build within us a sense of godly heritage and spiritual identity. I.e. they help define who we are. Third, just because you get older doesn't mean that you get tired of them or don't need to hear them anymore. Ancient stories from the Bible continue to remind me of the big picture of things, and I will cherish them until my last day on earth.

Practice Your Memory Skills

We should not only read the text and meditate on it. We should memorize large sections of scripture. The psalmist says, "O how I love your law! It is my meditation all the day" (Psa 119:97). 2 Timothy 3:14-17 says, *"But as for you, continue in what you have learned and have firmly believed, knowing from whom you learned it and how from childhood you have been acquainted with the sacred writings, which are able to make you wise for salvation through faith in Christ Jesus. All Scripture is breathed out by God and profitable for teaching, for reproof, for correction, and for training in righteousness, that the man of God may be competent, equipped for every good work."*

With the technology available in the modern world, people today are much more deficient in their memory skills than those in ages past. Before print and digital media became a prominent part of life, people had to remember a whole repository of information that they would pass down to the next generation. This includes details of stories, genealogies, and moral instruction that would be transmitted largely by word of mouth.

I have found that when I have to memorize something really important, I internalize it better, and I take more interest in it. Don't allow your memory skills to hibernate. Exercise them. If you work hard at it, your ability to memorize will actually improve. Use mnemonic devices, play word association games, recite, and even sing. All these techniques will help you become a better student. And when you work hard at memorizing God's Word, you will be amazed at how addicting (in a good way) learning will become.

The Sky is the Limit

This process never stops, as long as there is life, breath, and the desire to grow. When it comes to the business of learning the things of God, failure is not an option. "But grow in the grace and knowledge of our Lord and Savior Jesus Christ. To him be the glory both now and to the day of eternity. Amen" (2 Pet 3:18). Toward that end, "Do your best to present yourself to God as one approved, a worker who has no need to be ashamed, rightly handling the word of truth" (2 Tim 2:15). Make reading and studying a lifelong pursuit, so that even when you are old, you are still learning new things, still growing, and still striving for the "upward call of God in Christ Jesus" (Phil 3:14).

I love you very much!

Papa Mike

Questions

1. Do we learn more if we have an interest in the topic? If so, what are some ways that we can make learning fun?

2. Most people never reach their full potential in life. Why is this so?

3. What are some things you can do to increase your motivation to learn?

4. What are some keys to getting more interested in learning spiritual things?

2. Love God with All Your Heart

Steve Klein

My Dear Grandchildren,

I have loved you with all my heart from the moment you were born. But there is Someone who has loved you longer and more deeply than I ever could. He loved you before time began. And He wants nothing more than for you to love Him back…forever! Let me tell you about His love for you, and how wonderful it would be for you to love Him with all your heart your whole life long.

God Loves You

God loves you more than you or I can really understand. The apostle Paul prayed that Christians would "know the love of Christ that surpasses knowledge" (Eph 3:17-19). That's a little puzzling, isn't it? How can you know something that's beyond knowing? Sounds hard!

Can you wrap you mind around the idea that someone loved you so much that He asked His only child to die for you? That's what God did! "God **so** loved the world that He gave His only begotten Son" (John 3:16). Just put your name in place of the word "world" in that verse and think about what God did for you! God so loved *Clayton*. God so loved *Eden*. God so loved *Steven*.

God didn't do that because you were deserving of it. In fact, once you are of age, you will deserve punishment for your sins, just like the rest of the world. "But God demonstrates His own love toward us, in that while we were still sinners, Christ died for us" (Rom 5:8). That makes God's love even more amazing. It's one thing to ask, "Why would anyone pay for the deliverance of a human being with the blood of His own child?" But the more difficult question is, "Who would pay to redeem a sinful, rebellious child with the blood of a perfect child?" God took His perfect, sinless Son and sacrificed Him to save you! We don't fully understand it. But this much we can say for certain: *You must be very precious to Him; He loves you "so."*

As hard as it is to fathom the *depth* of God's love, its *length* is a dimension that may be just as difficult to understand. Just *how long* has God loved us? Well, He says that He loved the children of Israel with "an everlasting love" (Jer 31:3). In other words, He has loved His children outside the bounds of time itself. "He chose us in Him before the foundation of the world" (Eph 1:4). He decided before the world was ever created that He loved us so much that His Beloved Son would become a sacrificial Lamb, slain for our redemption. Jesus is described as "the Lamb slain from the foundation of the world," and we are told that His sacrifice was "foreordained before the foundation of the world, but was manifest in these last times for **you**" (Rev 13:8; 1 Pet 1:20).

What it all boils down to is that God loves you immensely and eternally. He will *never* stop loving you. The value of this truth was graphically illustrated in the life of a man named George Matheson. Mr. Matheson became blind in his mid-twenties, at which point he was dumped by the girl he planned to marry; she refused to be tied down in a life-long relationship to a blind man. She just didn't love him. A few years later, on the evening of his own sister's wedding, George Matheson remembered that painful break-up; as he pondered on the memory and contemplated the love of God, he was moved to write a hymn:

"O Love that will not let me go,
I rest my weary soul in thee;
I give thee back the life I owe,
That in thine ocean depths its flow may richer, fuller be."

Despite having been betrayed and abandoned by the love of a human, Mr. Matheson knew that God loved him so much that He would never let him go or forsake him. The lyrics of the song suggest that when we surrender our lives to God, we are merely returning to Him the love that He has lavished so richly upon us. "We love Him because He first loved us" (1 John 4:19).

God Wants You to Love Him

God's *love* gives us good reason to love Him, but God's *word* informs us that we must love Him. Long ago, God gave the Israelites this commandment: "Hear, O Israel: The LORD our God, the LORD is one! You shall love the LORD your God with all your heart, with all your soul, and with all your strength" (Deut 6:4-5). These words form what the Jews call the *Shema*, which is the Hebrew word translated *Hear* at the beginning of the passage. To the Jews, this statement was and is the greatest commandment—the very foundation of their religion. It needs to be the foundation of your entire life!

In Mark 12:28, Jesus is asked, "Which commandment is the most important of all?" Jesus responds by quoting the *Shema*: "The most important is, 'Hear, O Israel: The Lord our God, the Lord is one. And you shall love the Lord your God with all your heart and with all your soul and with all your mind and with all your strength" (Mark 12:20-30, ESV). In Matthew's account, Jesus calls this "the first and great commandment" (Matt 22:38). Loving God with your entire being is at once both the most important thing and the greatest thing you will ever do.

As you grow up and make your way into the adult world, many things will vie for your affection. There will be pleasures and people and possessions that attract you. Be careful not to love anything or anyone more than God. "Keep your heart with all diligence, for out of it spring the issues of life" (Prov 4:23). Don't get so tied up in your education, or your work, or your social activities that you don't have time for God, because if you don't have *time* for Him, it means you don't have *love* for Him.

Love God by Putting Him First

Think with me for a moment about what God was saying to Israel in the first three of the ten commandments:

- *You shall have no other gods before me (Exo 20:3).*
- *You shall not make for yourself a carved image (Exo 20:4).*
- *You shall not take the name of the LORD your God in vain (Exo 20:7).*

The Lord wants the exclusive adoration and respect of His children! He is a jealous God (Exo 20:5). Our affection for Him must surpass every worldly desire or attachment. The New Testament puts it this way: "Do not love the world or the things in the world. If anyone loves the world, the love of the Father is not in him. For all that is in the world—the lust of the flesh, the lust of the eyes, and the pride of life—is not of the Father but is of the world" (1 John 2:15-16).

I very much want you to find fulfillment and happiness. The world will never provide that because, no matter how much you love it, it will never really love you back. But, when you "know the love of Christ which passes knowledge" you will "be filled with all the fullness of God" (Eph. 3:19). And when you are filled with the fulness of God you are FULFILLED to the brim and running over! Your life will find its meaning and purpose in loving Him.

Love God through Obedience

I need to warn you about something. There will be people in your life who try to convince you that you can love God without obeying God. In fact, most of the world, including many folks who call themselves Christians, believe this. IT IS A LIE FROM THE DEVIL! The Bible repeatedly teaches that loving God and keeping His commandments go hand in hand. Just look at these declarations from God's word:

- *If you love me, you will keep my commandments (John 14:15).*
- *If you keep My commandments, you will abide in My love, just as I have kept My Father's commandments and abide in His love (John 15:10).*
- *For this is the love of God, that we keep his commandments. And His commandments are not burdensome (1 John 5:3).*
- *If anyone loves me, he will keep my word, and my Father will*

> *love him, and we will come to him and make our home with him (John 14:23).*
> - *Whoever does not love me does not keep my words (John 14:24).*

This truth is made *so plain* in Scripture that you would think no one would ever be fooled into thinking otherwise. But many are fooled. Don't let yourself become one of them! Loving God means having the attitude "Speak Lord, your servant hears!" It means that you are so devoted to God and so determined to please Him that His every wish is your command, and His every command becomes your wish.

Love God through Worship

When you were a toddler, your Oma and I so enjoyed receiving your "sugar." That's what we called your sweet hugs and kisses. God loves to be on the receiving end of your affection as well. Worship is a way for you to express your love to Him. In fact, the word that is most often translated "worship" in the New Testament literally means to *kiss* or *adore*. It is important to remember that when you are worshiping God, you are showing Him your love.

When you give a loved one a gift, you don't give something that you want; you give something that will please the one you love. As you got older and began to express yourself in words, Oma and I have often given you gifts for your birthday or for Christmas that we knew you would enjoy; we knew because you would tell us over and over again what you were wishing for! Even so, God has told us what He wants from us in worship.

Let's always make sure that we are giving Him what He has asked for, and not just something that pleases us. God will not be pleased with just any old thing you want to give Him. Show Him you love Him by considering His wishes. "Walk prudently when you go to the house of God; and draw near to hear rather than to give the sacrifice of fools, for they do not know that they do evil" (Eccl 5:1).

The religious world is constantly coming up with innovative ways of worship designed to please people—often with little regard for God's expressed wishes. For instance, God tells us to "Speak to each other with psalms, hymns, and spiritual songs, singing and making music in your hearts to the Lord" (Eph. 5:19, NCV). But people like to hear guitars and drums and pianos and fiddles, so they bring in these instruments of music. They entertain themselves with tunes that sound a lot like pop music (or rock, or country, or bluegrass) when what God asked for was that we sing to each other and make the music in our hearts. Who do we really love when we worship according to our own wishes? Does God accept such worship? Jesus said, "In vain they worship me, teaching as doctrines the commandments of men" (Matt 15:9).

Showing love to God in worship involves much more than just giving Him *the form* of worship that He's asked for; remember that worship is an expression of *the love* that is in our hearts! This was the attitude King David was expressing when he said, "I will praise You with all my heart, Lord my God, and will honor Your name forever, for Your faithful love for me is great" (Psa 86:13, HCSB). This combination of *right action* and *right emotion* in worship is part of what Jesus is getting at in John 4:24 when He says, "God is spirit, and those who worship him must worship in spirit and truth."

Love God by Loving God's Children

Do you know how electricity works? It is made at a power plant that may be many miles from your home. It takes a lot of energy to make electricity. In our area, electricity is made with nuclear energy. Once electricity has been generated, it moves through power lines to your house. There is a lot of power in those electrical wires – enough to run all the lights, appliances and televisions in your house! The power runs through smaller wires in the walls of your house, and you access it by flipping a switch or plugging in to an outlet. When you turn on a light switch, it makes a connection between the wire that runs into your house and the wire that runs from the switch to the light. When the connection is made, the light comes on! But unless that connection is complete, the light will not come on. You could have all the power in the world coming to your house, but unless the electrical connection is complete, there will be no light.

God's love is the most powerful thing there is. It is more powerful than electricity or the nuclear energy that generates it. It is as if God has sent His love to you through a wire that is shaped like a cross. Remember, God *so loved you* that He gave His only begotten Son! But that love doesn't really light up your life until you share it with others. Loving others flips the switch in your heart that perfects or completes God's love within you. The Bible says that, "If we love one another, God abides in us, and His love has been perfected in us" (1 John 4:12).

So, loving God means loving others also. "Beloved, if God so loved us, we also ought to love one another" (1 John 4:11). If you love your brother you will demonstrate it in certain ways. For instance, you will be longsuffering and forgiving (Eph. 4:2). You will abstain from doing or saying anything that could cause your brother to sin because, "He who loves his brother abides in the light, and there is no cause for stumbling in him" (1 John 2:10). And, you will freely give to your brother to alleviate his needs (1 John 3:16-18). But something else you will do (and this is very important) is that you will consistently assemble with your brethren for worship, because that is a way of expressing your love for God and a means of encouraging more love in others! The Bible says, "And let us consider how to stir up one another to love and good works, not neglecting to meet together, as is the habit of some, but encouraging one another..." (Heb. 10:24-25, ESV). If you truly love God and His people, you will make it a lifelong habit to assemble with God's people for worship.

Someday this life will be over for us. If things follow their natural order, I will depart before you do, but you will come along soon enough. When a person dies, his love of earthly things also perishes (Eccl. 9:5-6). But the love of God is eternal. An old song asks the question, *"If love never lasts forever, what's forever for?"* Forever is for loving God!! If you and I have loved God in this life, we will be able to love Him together for eternity. God is eternal, and God is love.

Let's make a pact right now that we will love God with every fiber of our being as we live on earth, so that we can be together in heaven where we will "live and love an eternity through." This hope fills me with unspeakable joy! I can almost see us there together before God's throne, and you will be my "crown of rejoicing...in the presence of our Lord Jesus Christ" (1 Thess 2:19).

Love God! Heaven awaits!

With all my heart,

from Papa to Clayton, Eden and Steven

Questions

1. Why is it difficult to understand the depth of the love God has for us?

2. Why is it impossible to find lasting fulfillment by loving the things of the world?

3. How does genuine love for God shape the way we worship Him?

4. How do the gifts we give to others reflect our love or lack thereof?

5. Why does love for your brother motivate you to walk in the light?

3. Love Your Neighbor as Yourself

Wilson Adams

Dear Grandchildren:

This is the most exciting writing assignment I have ever had. –To share with you some lessons God has given me in my sixty years on His earth. By the way, I have no grand[father] illusions that you will "get" this as you grow through your teenage years. In fact, if you are like most teens, you won't exactly be looking for advice from older people in this phase of your life. However, my hope is that one day you will remember this book and find comfort in these chapters. Who knows, you may find a smile moment of connection to a grandfather who loves you dearly.

The Rule

I know "rules" aren't always fun to follow, but get used to them. Truth is, there will never be a time in your life when you won't have to follow some rules. This one is tops.

*Treat people the same way you want them to treat you...*Matthew 7:12

It may be the most famous statement Jesus ever made. People who know little about the Bible can usually quote what is referred to as the *Golden Rule*. However, it's one thing to quote it; it's another thing to live it.

Live it! It will change your life.

Embracing these simple words will enable you to reach the summit of life. I've heard this verse called, "The Everest of Ethics." Hopefully you were paying attention in school and learned that Mount Everest is the world's tallest mountain. The point? You don't have to spend a lot of money going to seminars and buying books on how to succeed in life and get along with people. The secret to life success is summed up in a single sentence: treat others the way you want to be treated. That's it! By the way, if you dare to climb this mountain, you will be rewarded with a view that is out-of-this-world!

During the first half of your life you probably won't think much about how to spend the second half. You'll be too busy getting through school, getting through college, getting a job, getting married, getting a house, and getting all the stuff to put in it. That's a lot of "getting"—and that's okay. It's quite normal, really. But somewhere along the way of achieving, learning, and earning you will reach a plateau—kind of like a pullout on a trail with an eye-catching view. I'm not sure *when* you will reach it, but you will and you will know.

At that point you will have cause to pause and ask a great question: *Is this all there is?* The answer? *No.* There is more and there is better—but only if you look up, look around, and get your eyes off yourself.

You see, the first half of your life will be filled with some amazing firsts. It's like receiving the opening football kickoff and all the excitement and cheering that goes with it. By the way, you will find the first half will go by faster than you think. And in the process (if you pay attention to God), you will discover your heart's holiest chamber. You will discover that everything you do is about *Him*—and allowing Him to direct your heart to helping others.

Therefore we have as our ambition...to be pleasing to Him. 2 Corinthians 5:9

The happiest people I know are those who have shifted their focus from being success-driven to becoming significance-driven. Regardless of the "selfie" generation, it really isn't all about you. The sooner you learn that basic truth, the better your life will be. I promise.

You must come to believe that what you ultimately leave behind will be more important than any other achievement. You can change the world and you can make it better. But first, *you* must change.

God gives to each of you a gift. Right now, I see in you the magic of childlike curiosity and imagination and am only just beginning to understand your unique gifts. Regardless of how God gifts you with talents and opportunities (and He will), you must do one thing above all else: you must open your gift and use it in service to others.

As each has received a special gift, employ it in serving one another as good stewards of the manifold [many folded] *grace of God.* 1 Peter 4:9

Open your gift and share it with others.

Who Is My Neighbor?

On one occasion, Jesus had a talk with a lawyer (Luke 9:25). Like most lawyers, he was good at asking tricky questions designed to trip up the defendant. To his credit, he came to the right source (Jesus) and asked the right question ("What shall I do to inherit eternal life?"). Jesus told him to love God and to "love your neighbor as yourself." Then the young man slipped into lawyer mode:

And wishing to justify himself, he said to Jesus, 'And who is my neighbor?'" Luke 10:29

Wishing to justify himself... That's always the temptation. –To find a loophole, an escape clause, an explanation that makes us look good. Jesus did not let him (or us) off that easily. Doing what He often did, He launched into a story that may be the most remembered of all: *The Good Samaritan* (vv. 30-37).

This story is about compassion and helping us understand what it means. Apparently, compassion is about passion-action or it is not compassion. The issue is not about "feeling bad" about hurting people; the issue is doing something about it. By the way, God is not asking you to do something He hasn't already done (Matt 14:14; John 3:16).

God's passion for you was more than a *feeling*. His passion led to His com-passion, which led to His act-tion. The message of Jesus' story is clear: *compassion* must be the go-to verb of your life. It's where your faith takes on flesh. After all, "it is more blessed to give than to receive." It's true.

As a result, compassion is more than you think because it is more than you can think (as in comprehend). But once you find it and use it, you won't ever be the same.

Back to the story...

I don't know much about the beaten man on the side of the road. I do know that evil had befallen him and he almost died. I know also that two very religious men happened along.

Decision

Each of these had the same opportunity. Perhaps the first two men (the Jewish priest and the Levite) viewed their God-work as above the fray of human misery. In other words, their occupation had become their *pre*occupation. After all, their work was holy and involved things like reading the scrolls, answering legal (Law of Moses) questions, preparing the sacrifices, and leading the temple worship.

They were important men doing important things that were time consuming and energy draining. After all, they had God places to be and God things to do. Ironically, in their attempt to do right things, they failed to do right things.

Like... love their neighbor.

I am sure their decision not to get involved made perfect sense (to them). On the other hand, it made no sense to the hurting man on the side of the road. I've always wondered—

- Did he see them pass by?
- Did he know who they were?
- Did they not hear his cries?
- If they didn't hear his cries, why did they cross the road?
- Was the hurting man struck with the irony of their hypocrisy?

Jesus doesn't tell us. Instead, He focuses on the one man who decided to do what he could (vv. 33-34). The fact that Jesus makes the Samaritan the hero of the story was shocking beyond belief. If any group was stereotyped as uneducated, unethical, and uncouth, it was the Samaritans. All of which says, if you are a follower of Jesus, racial prejudice must have no place in your life.

By the way, no one would ever remember the Good Samaritan if he only had good intentions. However, his compassion became passion-action (v.35).

I am stuck by three truths:

1. Compassion will measure your heart. It is interesting that the Samaritan did not pry into the hurting man's circumstances before rendering help. He didn't look down on the man lying in the dirt or lecture him on taking safer travel precautions. He also didn't immediately ask the man if he wanted a Bible study. What he did first was... *see* the man.

Rather than look *past* him, he went *to* him. The image of the hurting registered in his head, connected to his heart, and then led him to bend down and touch him with his hands. At that moment, nothing else mattered. Rather than worry about what he couldn't do, he decided to do what he could.

2. Compassion will interrupt your plans. Do you think the Samaritan had nothing else to do? Like the priest and the Levite, he also had places to go and things to do. Compassion is seldom convenient. I am reminded of the saying: *Life is what happens to you while you're busy making other plans.* The same is true regarding compassion.

3. Compassion will cost you. It cost him. It cost him time, energy, and money. I'm guessing the priest and Levite knew that, too. But they decided the hurting man wasn't worth the expenditure.

Sadly, some want to follow a Jesus who calls them into a life of comfort and convenience. They want a Jesus who demands little and asks for the same. They want a Jesus who fills their head with a lot of Bible knowledge that translates into very little heart compassion. That is not the Jesus you are called to follow.

Go and Do the Same

I don't know who wrote this, but I want you to let these words soak into your heart.

I saw what I saw and I can't forget it.
I heard what I heard and I can't ignore it.
I know what I know and I can't deny it.

Something on the road has cut me to my soul.

Your pain has changed me.
Your dream has inspired me.
Your face a memory,
Your hope a fire.
Your courage asks me what I'm afraid of.
Your courage asks me what I am made of.

Most of all...
Your courage asks me what I know about God.

Go and do the same.

I don't know whom God will place in your path, but He will put someone there. Someone you can help; someone you can change. Don't miss the moment. For in life actions of compassion toward others, you will find meaning in your own. "Cast your bread on the surface of the waters, for you will find it after many days" (Eccl 11:1). That's poetry and another way of saying: *It's more blessed to give than to receive.* It's true.

Crazy Love

I am flooded today with memories of one year ago. We were given a week to pack and catch a plane to the other side of the world (ancient Macedonia). Your grandmother and I had made a life-changing decision. As fifty-something empty nesters, we were adopting a sibling group of three from an orphanage in Bulgaria.

"Your what?" "Adoption?" "Are you crazy?"

Truthfully, there have been times we've wondered the same.

Second-guessing is a given when entering uncharted territory of any great adventure. Then you do an amazing thing: you take a deep breath and climb on.

By the way, it's easier to look away. In fact, the first two days we spent at the orphanage, we looked away, too. It was just too painful. -The hollow eyes. -The looks of hopelessness. -The sorrowful stares at the strangers from America.

We live in a broken world.

Over 1,000,000 (million) children are forced into slavery or sex trafficking. Over 1,000,000,000 (billion) people on our planet live in extreme poverty—making less than $2 per day. 16,000 children die every day from starvation and/or preventable disease.

That's a lot of zeros.

Yet each one of them represents a life—a life worth saving and a life for which Jesus died.

It's easy for Americans to live behind comfortable earth tones of rose-colored glasses. It's easy to assume everyone has it as easy as do we. It's easy to think that all kids have a childhood like yours and mine. It's easy to look the other way because looking at the real problem makes us very uncomfortable.

Maybe we should take off our glasses and get a heavy dose of world reality.

The numbers don't lie.

- There are over 150 million orphans worldwide.
- 250,000 kids are adopted annually (good news) while 14 million age out annually with no family, no roots, no home, and nowhere to go other than the streets (tragic news).
- 60% of orphaned infants in China never live to see their childhood.
- 60% of the orphan girls in Eastern Europe age out and go into prostitution.
- 70% of the orphan boys in Eastern Europe age out and go into gangs.
- 10% of orphan boys and girls who age out commit suicide during their first year on the streets.
- The Dave Thomas Foundation for adoption reports that only 9,000 international kids are adopted annually and that number is declining.
- The average age of a waiting child is 7-8 years old.

If they stood shoulder to shoulder, the orphans of the world would form a line around the United States—not once, or twice, but four times! In other words, each day our Father sees a line of vulnerable children—harassed, helpless, and hopeless—stretching 30,000 miles long.

Each of them deserves a chance. One noted, "Orphans are easier to ignore before you know their names. They are easier to ignore before you see their faces. It's easier to pretend they're not real before you hold them in your arms. But once you do, everything changes."

In the process, you will also change.

Your Macedonian Call

This is where all of us struggle. Feeling overwhelmed by the numbers, we are left facing three reactions:

1. We look away. The orphan crisis is right in front of our eyes, but only if we are willing to see. Sadly, out of sight and out of mind becomes our easy go-to while, simultaneously, we gather to worship, sing songs about Jesus, hear about the Good Samaritan, and pray for opportunities to help others. Then we go out to eat and on to the rest of our week with little thought (or intention) to actually *do* what our faith demands.

Like the priest and Levite, we miss the point of what true religion is all about. Thankfully, Jesus did not look the other way. He believed each of us were worth saving.

2. We decide that because we can't do everything, we will do nothing. Not only is that not a very good strategy, it's not a biblical one. This is where you must come to terms with the most critical number of all: the power of one. It only takes one to change the life of one. Before you become overwhelmed by the magnitude of the problem, it only takes one family to change the life of one orphan. That makes the number "one" the most important number of all.

God cares passionately about the fatherless (Psa 27:10; 68:5-6; 82:3-4; Hos 14:3). Come to think of it, all Christians should have a heart for adoption since all of us are adopted (Rom 8:15; Eph 1:5).

That's why we "visit the fatherless" (James 1:27). While not everyone can adopt (or should), everyone can do something. Like what?

- Work to foster a culture that embraces adoption.
- Pray for the fatherless.
- Give resources (time and money) to groups like *Sacred Selections*—providing placement of the fatherless into the homes of Christians.
- Attend a *Sacred Selections* event and learn more ways that you can be involved.
- Adopt an adopting family by giving encouragement and support.

One thing is certain, a church that doesn't welcome the orphan into the assembly, won't welcome the sinner into the baptistery. This is evangelism 101. It is walking into enemy territory and taking what Satan has decided is already his.

3. We do what we can with what we have. It is the Mary Principle: "She has done what she could" (Mark 14:8). That's all any of us can do. Truthfully, that's all God asks. The Samaritan couldn't solve all the problems of his world. He couldn't solve political corruption, race issues, or fix the crime problem. What he could do was stop and help his neighbor. He did what he could.

Do you have a heart for the least of these? In the words of another poet,

Turn away—it's the easiest thing to do.
But what if...it was only up to you?

Would you take a stand, would you reach your hand?
Would you give them something to hold on to?

This is not the only way to open your gift and give back, but is is one way. It is the way your grandparents have chosen. Dearest Callie Rose, Gavin, Cal, Drake, Brody—and to those I have yet to meet—I hope you will treasure this book. All these chapters are from the hearts of some amazing men—grandfathers all. I love you and I hope you will be as proud of me as I am of you. Thanks to Callie Rose, you know me as, "Beba" (where that came from, I do not know). But it has stuck and it's okay. Nana and I pray that you will follow Jesus and reach out to the hurting. Not only can you change their lives, they will change yours.

Questions

1. Why do you think Jesus' life rule ("Treat people the same way you want them to treat you...") is easier preached than practiced?

2. "It is more blessed to give than to receive..." (Acts 20:35). In what way(s) does the giver become the receiver?

3. What do you see as the difference between being success-driven and being significance-driven? *Follow up:* As you mature in life, discuss ways you can move from one to the other.

4. Luke 10:29—"But wishing to justify himself, he said to Jesus, 'And who is my neighbor?'" How was he seeking to justify himself?

5. Discuss ways the story of the Good Samaritan should impact our lives.

6. How do you define "compassion" and in what ways will it cost you?

7. What three reactions do we tend to have toward the orphan crisis? *Follow up:* Why are the first two not good options?

8. Why should adoption be close to the heart of the Christian?

9. Left high and dry by low tide, a little girl was tossing starfish back into the surf. An old man scowled and said, "Little girl, you can't possibly make a difference to all those starfish—there are thousands of them!" The little girl wasn't phased. She merely bent down, picked up another, and threw it back into the water. Looking at the old man, she said, "I made a difference to that one." The old man smiled. He then joined her in throwing back as many as they could. What do you think is the moral of the story?

4. Love Your Enemies

C. G. "Colly" Caldwell

Dear Zac, Jake, and Rhett,

I am so very blessed to have you as my three grandsons. And I am blessed that each of you is strong but kind. One of the most rewarding traits of character you can learn as a young man is to be willing to forgive others and put aside differences even if you have been hurt in the process. And if others consider themselves your enemies, try never to do them harm in return. Jesus would call that, "Love your enemies." He said, "You have heard that it was said, 'You shall love your neighbor and hate your enemy. But I say to you, love your enemies, bless those who curse you, do good to those who hate you, and pray for those who spitefully use you and persecute you, that you may be sons of your Father in heaven; for He makes His sun rise on the evil and on the good, and sends rain on the just and on the unjust." (Matthew 5:43-45).

I say I am blessed because if any of you has an enemy, I don't know about it. Oh, I'm sure you may have had a scuffle or two with neighbor kids or some disputes at school with other students like all boys and girls do. I wouldn't deny that, but those kinds of things go away, usually by the next day.

Perhaps one of the most common opportunities for young unmarried like yourselves to have an "enemy" is with a girlfriend or boyfriend who decides at this age to move on. That may leave you heartbroken but it doesn't have to result in becoming an "enemy." My grandson's girlfriend would be acting foolishly and ignorantly while not knowing what she is giving up, mind you. But it has happened once or twice to my recollection, and it almost certainly leaves hurt feelings toward each other. I must say it happened to me a couple of times, too. The thing to remember in that case and many others where you think you have an enemy is that God may be working out something far better for the future. If you have the right attitude, it will be even better in the end. Of course, a girlfriend, a friend, or anyone else doesn't have to become an enemy, even if you may not want to be around that person much any more after he/she has hurt you.

So, how should you treat people who hurt you? I know that you are concerned not only about what will "work;" i.e., what will be to your advantage and make your life comfortable. Because you have a relationship with the Lord and want to do what is right, you are also concerned about what Jesus would do. So, what does God's word teach about this?

Let's go back to the 5 W questions of basic information gathering that we all learn in high school: **Who?, What?, Where?, When?, Why? And then, of course, we will add "How?"** Answers to these questions can be valuable in Bible study as well as in writing term papers, in legal or law-enforcement fact finding, in historical research, or in news reporting, and a host of other types of activities we engage in every day. So stay with me on this!

WHO? The Merciful and Peacemaker Disciples

Jesus spoke the words in Matthew 5 which include His teaching that all should "Love your enemies," in what we call the Sermon on the Mount. Do you remember how that message is introduced to us?

> And seeing the multitudes, He went up on a mountain, and when He was seated His disciples came to Him. Then He opened His mouth and taught them, saying: "Blessed are the poor in spirit, For theirs is the kingdom of heaven. Blessed are those who mourn, for they shall be comforted. Blessed are the meek, for they shall inherit the earth. Blessed are those who hunger and thirst for righteousness, for they shall be filled. Blessed are the merciful, for they shall obtain mercy. Blessed are the pure in heart, for they shall see God. Blessed are the peacemakers, for they shall be called sons of God. Blessed are those who are persecuted for righteousness' sake, for theirs is the kingdom of heaven. Blessed are you when they revile and persecute you, and say all kinds of evil against you falsely for My sake. Rejoice and be exceedingly glad, for great is your reward in heaven, for so they persecuted the prophets who were before you" (Matt 5:1-12).

It appears that Jesus was speaking directly to his "disciples," but His message was obviously intended to instruct the "multitudes." Jesus knew that not all people would love their enemies. It just wouldn't happen. But He was appealing to those who would be His disciples and take on a certain kind of character. Who would they be? They would be those who act mercifully (v. 7). They would be peacemakers (v. 9). They would have enemies (v. 11) but they would be the ones who rejoice looking forward to a reward in heaven while understanding their relationship to God (v. 12).

WHAT? Love Your Enemy

An "enemy" is one who has hostile and offensive feelings of evil intent against another. He or she may express those feelings in openly harmful, aggressive actions. Those can become abusive and even violent. They can harm our reputations and hinder us from achieving goals we have set for ourselves. We may have to even be physically careful around them.

The Greek word for "love" in Jesus' moral teaching is most often *agapé*. "Loving" in this sense does not necessarily require "liking." It does, however, require doing good to others. It means we will always try to do what is right and what is in the best interest of those we are to love.

Sometimes people can be very obnoxious and hateful in their dealings with us. Of course, there are probably going to be efforts to do harm to you grandsons as you get older and establish adult relationships. It is important to learn how to treat others while we are young because those lessons will go with us through life. Being kind toward those who abuse us is a "life-lesson."

As we said, we want to be like Jesus. So what did Jesus and his followers do? On the cross, Jesus said, "Father, forgive them, for they do not know what they do" (Luke 23:34). He could have called for God to strike them dead or violently stop their aggression against Him. As strange as it may seem to us, however, Jesus considered His enemies to be among the ones He came to save. Another example is Stephen, the first Christian to be martyred. He said as they were stoning him to death, "Lord, do not charge them with this sin" (Acts 7:60). We do not know if he actually heard Jesus make His appeal from the cross, but he must have heard about it and wanted to imitate Jesus. And Paul made the following statement in the final chapter of his second letter to Timothy in which he believed that he would soon die, "At my first defense no one stood with me, but all forsook me. May it not be charged against them" (2 Tim 4:16).

These may seem to have been extreme examples, but they tell us what we should do in any circumstance. The girlfriend/boyfriend illustration is probably only a fleeting or temporary example, as much as it hurts at the time. But sometimes young men and women can become very cruel and turn on one another damaging reputations through lies and schemes to get back at one another. We have even heard of suicides resulting from such cases. There are also bullies and negative persons at any age who just seem to try our patience and sometimes really do something or say something that hurts us deeply. Perhaps a more lasting example occurs if trouble arises a bit later in your marriage. It is always sad when spouses fight with each other and become enemies in the same household. Remember, we are to "love" our mates as Christ loved the church and gave himself for it" (Eph 5:25) even when we are hurt in our own families. And there will be people in our occupations who for whatever reason turn against us. Almost anyone in any relationship of life can provide the opportunity for us to experience enemies.

The most aggressive enemies of Jesus we read about in the Bible were those who claimed to be servants of God, the religious leaders of His own time and nation...the Pharisees, Sadducees, chief priests, and elders who led the spiritual thought and activities of His day. They, like Saul of Tarsus, thought they were serving God even when their actions attempting to hinder His mission and work were contemptible. It was that group who would test His teaching that all should "love your enemies!" They ultimately put Him to death, yet they were offered forgiveness by the loving Savior. Peter said, "Let all the house of Israel know assuredly that God has made this Jesus, whom you crucified, both Lord and Christ." And then he said, "Repent and let every one of you be baptized in the name of Jesus Christ for the remission of sin" (Acts 2:36-38).

WHERE?

Wherever God makes the sun to rise and the rain to fall

So "where" does God want us to love our enemies? Everywhere. In our homes, on the job, at school, everywhere, not just in the church. Remember Jesus on the cross and Stephen being stoned. Even when the enemy is at his worst, we are to love him. Jesus was forgiving and understanding of his enemies even on the cross.

Even if you were a slave on a plantation suffering all kinds of abuses, Jesus would say, "Love your enemies." When Peter was counseling servants on how to follow Jesus, he said, "Servants, be submissive to your masters with all fear, not only to the good and gentle, but also to the harsh. For this is commendable, if because of conscience toward God one endures grief, suffering wrongfully. For what credit is it if, when you are beaten for your faults, you take it patiently? But when you do good and suffer for it, if you take it patiently, this is commendable before God. For to this you were called, because Christ also suffered for us, leaving us an example, that you should follow His steps: who committed no sin nor was guile found in His mouth, who when He was reviled, did not revile in return, when he suffered, He did not threaten, but committed Himself to Him who judges righteously" (1 Pet 2:18-23).

WHEN? When Enemy Has Needs

Loving one's enemies is not an issue beginning with New Testament teaching. The Israelites were taught to love their enemies as well, particularly when your enemy has a need of some kind.

"If your enemy is hungry, give him bread to eat; and if he is thirsty, give him water to drink: for so you will heap coals of fir on his head and the Lord will reward you" (Prov 25:21-22).

If you meet your enemy's ox or his donkey going astray, you shall surely bring it back to him again. If you see the donkey of one who hates you lying under its burden, and you would refrain from helping it, you shall surely help him with it" (Exod 23:4-5).

Joseph is a great example in the way he treated his brothers who had done him great harm. Moses said, "You shall not take vengeance, nor bear any grudge against the children of your people, but you shall love your neighbor as yourself" (Lev 19:18).

WHY? Primarily because God has loved and forgiven us

In a companion passage, and perhaps on another occasion, Luke tells us that Jesus said, "Love your enemies, do good, and lend hoping for nothing in return; and your reward will be great, and you will be sons of the Most High. For He is kind to the unthankful and evil. Therefore, be merciful, just as your Father also is merciful" (Luke 6:27-36).

Loving and forgiving go together. Jesus told a story about a man who would not forgive when he had been forgiven. When his master who had forgiven him much more learned of it, he punished him severely. The message of the story is stated when Jesus said, "So my heavenly Father also will do to you if each of you, from his heart, does not forgive his brother his trespasses" (Matt 18:35).

Boys, you want to remember that God has loved and forgiven you, even though you have sinned against Him. That is why you should forgive others. But there is one other matter that you might want to consider. Maybe the one who has become your enemy did not have bad intentions or evil motives in what they did that hurt us? Sometimes hurt results from unintended actions or misspoken comments.

People don't always understand the implications of their actions. The one's who killed Jesus didn't get it (Luke 23:34; Acts 3:17; 1 Cor 2:8). And perhaps the person was having a bad day or was not feeling well or had been ill. Perhaps there was something going on in his/her life that resulted in a temporary negative attitude leading to things they really didn't mean. Perhaps we may not have understood. The fault may have been partly ours for failing to have compassion. There are all kinds of reasons to give another the benefit of the doubt, particularly if they become sorry for what they have done. Remember, Jesus loved His enemies even in the most severe time of his suffering at their hands.

HOW? Doing Good and Forgiving

Jesus gave some very practical guidelines when His teaching about loving our enemies was repeated in Luke. "But I say to you who hear: Love your enemies, do good to those who hate you. Bless those that curse you, and pray for them that spitefully use you. To him who strikes you on the one cheek, offer the other also. And from him who takes away your cloak, do not withhold your tunic either...." "But love your enemies, do good, and lend hoping for nothing in return; and your reward will be great, and you will be sons of the Most High. For He is kind to the unthankful and evil. Therefore, be merciful, just as your Father also is merciful" (Luke 6:27-36).

From this passage we learn three great lessons. Loving enemies involves doing good to them even when you don't feel like it. Loving enemies involves forgiving the wrongs done to you. Loving enemies involves not requiring that they reciprocate.

Now you guys will probably think after all this that I am going to say something very strange in closing this letter and here it is: The goal is to ELIMINATE our enemies. Funny? Well, of course I don't mean kill them. What I mean is that we should act so they will not be enemies any more. Work hard to reduce the list of those that you have something against by doing good to them. And then we should EXECUTE. I'm not saying put them to death. I'm saying that we should put into practice the teaching of Jesus that will be most productive in helping our enemies. We should want to help them by meeting their needs. By following Christ's lead, we also may be instrumental in leading them to Christ.

God bless you in your lives. You are among the greatest blessings in your Mimi's and Coggy's lives. And we pray for you especially in your spiritual lives. Always stay close to your family, love everyone, and be faithful to God and Christ. We love each of you with all our hearts.

"Coggy"

Questions

1. Identify your enemies. How did they become your enemies?

2. Why do you think bullies act as they do?

3. Why would someone say something hurtful about you that is not true?

4. How (specifically) does God want us to actually treat our

5. Stay True to the Word

David Carrozza

Wow! Look at you growing up so fast. I remember the first time I saw you beautiful face and realized what a miracle you are. So perfect, so complete, so helpless, so innocent and so much potential. Honey and I were so overwhelmed in that moment seeing you, a brand new life and imagining the journey you've just begun.

You, like me, didn't know this at your moment of birth, and even now you're just beginning to understand that you have been "marvelously and wonderfully made," formed and equipped with everything you need to be in our Father's image and fully pleasing to Him. This means, among other things, that your mind, body and spirit are capable of filling the purpose for which you were made. And as you will see in what I hope to share with you now, it is His WORD that will explain to you what that purpose is.

Honey and I love you more than you can know, and most likely you will not understand this until you have children and grandchildren of your own. It is a marvelous part of life that awaits you in the future and I hope my thoughts and God's word will help light the path that you are beginning to walk.

One of your first sensations is hearing, and one of the first things you hear is your mother's beating heart and the muffled sounds of her voice. It's a voice that will soothe you, sing to you, teach you, laugh with you, correct you, and slowly build your character. It is a voice you have come to love, to trust, and to obey. As time goes by, it is also a voice you will hear in your mind and remind you of her even long after your mother's life has ended. Learn to listen to it and treasure it in your heart. It won't be there forever.

You had to wait to hear the second most important voice in your life—your father's voice. Strong, assuring and confident, it is a different voice and plays a different role in your life. It is often the voice of teaching, the voice of instruction and discipline. It is the voice that protects you from physical and spiritual dangers. It is the voice of vigilance that anticipates harmful circumstances and relationships long before you can see or understand them. It is a voice you will question and disagree with at times. Even though your father's voice is different and sometimes difficult, you see it is a voice that comes from the same place as your mother's and your mother's heart—a heart full of love for you. Learn to respect your father's voice and as years pass your respect will grow into deeper love and appreciation for the wisdom of your fathers voice.

By now you have heard many voices in your growing world: voices of your brothers and sisters, voices of friends at school, the voices of teachers, preachers and coaches the crazy voices on social media, tweets, posts and snapchats, voices on television from celebrities and sports heroes, voices of authority at school and in government. So many voices! So much noise! So many different messages!

By now you know it is hard to control what you hear, but you can control who or what you listen to. And that is what I want to share. Will you listen?

Do you remember how proud you were when you first learned your

ABC's? Remember how mom and dad and how Honey and I clapped for you and ran over for a big ole' hug? Remember when you said your first Bible memory verse and we all celebrated and took you out for ice cream? It seems so elementary and simple now doesn't it? But here is where my little lesson begins.

Those ABC's and Bible verses are the building blocks for everything you have learned up to now. They will also continue to be the very same things, concepts, and principles that you will keep building on for the rest of your life. You'll never get to a point where you won't need your ABC's any longer. There's no point in your life where 2+2 won't be four. And there's never a point in time where the moral, ethical, and spiritual principles you've been taught by the voices of mom, dad, grandparents and Bible school teachers won't be true and apply to you. I hope you're thinking of the song you learned a few years ago, "The wise man built his house upon a rock…" Yes, it's those ABC's of Bible verses, Bible characters, and Bible stories that are the building blocks of a firm, rock solid, foundation.

When you learned your ABC's your discovered the code for knowledge. Everything you've comprehended up until now and for the rest of your life will be based on remembering your ABC's. The principles in God's word that you've learned so far are also like ABC's, only they build something uniquely different and much more important. They build your character. Your character will play a very big role in the quality, joys, happiness, fulfillment, and rewards you will experience in life. Finally, how you spend your life will determine your destiny. Pretty impressive stuff comes from simply remembering your ABC's.

I hope you keep listening a little bit longer so I can share a few examples. These are some of poppa's favorite ABC's, my favorite building blocks that I've tried to build my life and Honey's on for a long time. They are the same ABC's I taught to your daddy when he was growing up, and I'm happy to say he listened to my voice when he was young like you.

On the day you were born I marveled at how beautiful and perfect you were—face all scrunched up, wrinkled, and screaming. You were a brand new life that just "popped" into this world. I also understood at this moment that God has given you everything you need to be a reflection of His image. You had everything it takes to be pleasing to Him, physically and mentally. He made you just like Adam and Eve to be a physical manifestation of His goodness seen, felt, and experienced in the world He also created. God also made us to be "fruitful" and to "multiply" that fruitfulness and fill the world with it. Good fruit and good work is what our heavenly Father wants us to produce and multiply.

What kind of fruit? Goodness, righteousness, and truth (Eph 5:9). Love, joy, peace, longsuffering, kindness, goodness, faithfulness, gentleness, self-control. (Gal 5:22-23). The apostle Paul goes on to say there is NO LAW in the history of the human race against these characteristics—this fruit. Never. These fruits will grow in your life when the seeds of the gospel are planted in your heart and mind. These seeds—these fruits are the ABC's the foundation and the structures your entire life needs to be built on; they are the rock that will stand the test of time and the tests of the life you will lead. Just like the ABC's, they never change and they are never not relevant to your growth, your knowledge, and your life.

What kind of work does God want you to do with your life? Once again the apostle sheds light on what you are created for. "For we [all of God's people] are His workmanship [remember God made you. You didn't just HAPPEN], created in Christ Jesus for good works, which God prepared beforehand [from the beginning] that we should walk in them [do them]" (Eph 2:10).

By now you've learned in school and at home that all of our work is held up to some standard. Your parents and your teachers have some expectations of what kind of work you should do and how to test the goodness or not-so-goodness of our efforts. In other words, your work is measured and judged. You're used to being graded with an A, B or C. How then does our heavenly Father judge our work—your work? Well, first of all He does tell us clearly what to expect, what work to do, and how we will be judged. Even Cain, the first child born, learned this lesson when he was not doing what God instructed him about the right kind of sacrifice. "So the Lord said to Cain, 'Why are you angry? Why has your countenance fallen? If you do well, will you not be accepted? And if you do not do well, sin lies at the door. And its desire is for you, but you should rule over it" (Gen 4:6-7).

Another apostle, this time it's Peter, lets us know that God has given us everything we need to know to be pleasing to Him. "...His divine power has given to us all things that pertain to life and godliness, through the knowledge of Him who called us by glory and virtue, by which have been given to us exceedingly great and precious promises, that through these you may be partakers of the divine nature [the image of God], having escaped the corruption that is in the world through lust" (2 Pet 1:3-4). Paul, too, talks to us about this: "All scripture is given by inspiration of God, and it profitable for doctrine, for reproof, for correction, for instruction in righteousness, that the man of God may be complete, thoroughly equipped for every good work" (2 Tim 2:16-17).

When Jesus describes the judgement scene in Matthew 25, He describes how the Father will separate the sheep (good) from the goats (bad). This is a little bit like your teacher telling you what questions will be on the test. In this case, Jesus is telling us what work and what fruit we are expected to do and produce. Let's take a careful, really careful look. Because like God told Cain, "If you do well, will you not be accepted?" [into heaven]. "When the Son of Man comes in His glory, and all the holy angels with Him, then He will sit on the throne of glory. All the nations will be gathered before Him, and He will separate them one from another, as a shepherd divides his sheep from the goats. And He will set the sheep on His right hand, but the goats on the left. Then the King will say to those on His right hand, 'Come, you blessed of My Father, inherit the kingdom prepared for you from the foundation of the world: for I was hungry and you have Me food; I was thirsty and you gave Me drink; I was a stranger and you took Me in; I was naked and you clothed me; I was sick and you visited Me; I was in prison and you came to Me'" (Matt 25:32-36).

Another good example of what is expected from us comes from the book of Hebrews. The writer begins in Hebrews chapter six by talking about ABC's, but he calls them "the elementary principles of Christ." He goes on to say, "Therefore, leaving the elementary principles of Christ, let us go on to perfection [or completeness], not laying again the foundation [relearning your ABC's]..." (Heb 6:1). The writer continues his thoughts in verses 9-12: "But beloved, we are confident of better things concerning you [meaning you are going on to perfection], yes things that accompany salvation, though we speak in this manner. For God is not unjust to forget your WORK and LABOR OF LOVE, which you have shown toward His name [remember the judgement scene in Matthew 25? If you did it to the least of these you did it to Me.] in that you have ministered to the saints, and do minister." We are expected to help other people. It is the work that the gospel tells us to do.

When John the apostle wrote the book of Revelation, he encourages us by saying, "And behold, I [Jesus] am coming quickly, and My reward is with Me, to give everyone according to his work." Isn't it great that we know what that work is and can be prepared to do it? So we are ready for the test!

No matter what you do in life, whether you are a brain surgeon, pilot, sales person, stay at home mom, preacher or business person, God's will for you is to be like Him, produce His good fruit and do His good work. Jesus says I am the way, no man comes to the Father except through Me. In the book of Acts written by Luke, he tells us that before we were called Christians we were called "followers of the Way." The Bible teaches us the way to be pleasing to our Father, to live the life He prepared for us, full of purpose, peace and joy. It is a life built on faith, hope and love. These principles and practices are the ABC's for everything we need in this life and the life to come.

Stay true to your spiritual ABC's. You can't add to the alphabet; neither can you take letters out of the alphabet. John the apostle sternly warns us not to add to or take away from the word of God (cf. Rev 22:18-19).

Well you've listened to Poppa long enough and I'm thankful for that. One last thing before I finish—I want you to listen to the voice of a very wise man: "My son, do not forget my law, But let your heart keep my commands; For length of days and long life And peace they will add to you; trust in the LORD with all your heart and lean not on your own understanding (Prov 3:1-12). When you have time read the entire chapter of Proverbs 3. The words expressed here will never fail you.

Honey and I love you so much. We have enjoyed every minute of your life and every occasion we have shared. If you build your life on the ABC's of God's word, we will never be separated from one another. Not in this life or the next life.

Jesus once said, "unless you are converted and become like little children—yes just like you were—you will by no means enter the kingdom of heaven" (Matt 18:4). Do you know what that means? It means that unless we TRUST and OBEY like children do their own father [and mother], we won't be pleasing to our heavenly Father.

Stay true to God's word. It will always be a light; it will always guide you to the right, and it will never fail you. It is the ROCK, the firm foundation.

All my love and prayers,

Poppa

Questions

1. List three ABC [basic] spiritual principles that have most influenced your behaviors and describe how or provide an example.

2. Think about the closest and best relationship you have with someone and describe as many spiritual principles or a "fruits of the spirit" that characterize and sustains it. For example "kindness" or "honesty".

3. Now describe what would happen to that relationship if you took out some of those characteristics and replaced it with its opposite. For example instead of kindness you replaced cruelty or gentleness with anger.

4. Think of a Bible character that demonstrates one of the foundational ABC Biblical principles in his/her life. For example Joseph demonstrated patience while waiting two years in prison after helping the butler and baker.

5. Just like the ABC's are the beginning of learning what does the Bible say is the ABC's or beginning of knowledge? What kind of knowledge or wisdom do you think this foundational principle build and develop? Why is this so important for everything in your / our lives?

6. What would happen to your reading, writing and understanding skills if you start taking out letters of the alphabet or starting including other additional letters in the alphabet or started replacing all of the "A's" and "L's" with some other letter? How would that effect your ability or read or someone else's ability to understand you? Now think about what happens to a person's life when they start taking out Biblical principles with

> **Training and Concern for Children**
>
> "Let your children be partakers of true Christian training. Let them learn that humility is of great avail with God." (Clement of Rome, c. AD 96)
>
> "Who is there that does not feel a greater concern for his children than for himself?" (Tertullian, c. AD 207)

6. Be Different

David Posey

Dear Lexi, Will, Kaia, Pierce, Amyla, Reichen and Griffin,

I'm guessing you can all remember the theme of camp in 2017, since you were all there. It was "Wired to be Weird." Will even designed the camp t-shirt you all wore. The key Bible passage was 1 Peter 2:9, "But you are a chosen race, a royal priesthood, a holy nation, a people for his own possession, that you may proclaim the excellencies of him who called you out of darkness into his marvelous light."

The theme emphasized the unique nature of those in God's world, his kingdom. You are "holy" (set apart) and, in the words of an older version of the passage, "a *peculiar* people." The theme was similar to a study that some of you participated in earlier in the year that we called, "The Joy of Being Different."

Wait! How can there be *joy* in being unlike everyone else around you??

That's a good question, and that's what I want to talk to you about. If we are all going to get to heaven some day, we'll do it because we set ourselves apart from a world that wants to make us just like everyone else.

But it's difficult. Being different than those around us is uncomfortable. It's true that some try to be different just to be different, because they want to draw attention to themselves or identify with a certain group. They might dress in certain clothing or get pierced or get a tattoo, trying to set themselves apart from the crowd. But, is that really being different? Aren't there 1,000s of people who have done that?

Some people like to dress in all black, with black fingernail polish and dark lipstick. Are they "different"? Not really. Most of her friends do the same thing; in fact, dressing like that has a name: it's called "Goth." It's a little unusual, but it's not really all that different.

My hope for each of you is that you will be different in a much more meaningful way: different, not just to be "different," but because *Jesus* is different.

Each of you is unique and special in your own way. Lexi, you are sensitive, sensible and kindhearted and have a unique ability to analyze things in a way that is mature beyond your years. Will, you have always been comfortable in your own skin, unfazed by what others think or say, yet still considerate of others. Kaia, you have a heart of gold, and have impressed us with your desire to help people who are less fortunate. Pierce, besides being a talented trumpet player, your Mimi and I love the way you pray; you are so thoughtful! Amyla, you are funny, athletic and modest. But you seem to know what you want and are willing to work hard for it. We love that kind of focus. Reichen, you are a great football player but we are most proud of you because you have channelled your terrible experience at Sandy Hook into a deep care for others who have endured similar trauma. And Griffin, you are our "renaissance man"; you have so many interests, it's hard to keep up. You like pets, plants, art, football, math and science. Your teachers love you and so do we.

All of you have special abilities and a unique "voice" that can be used to make a difference in this world. You each have something you can do that no one else can do just like you. I hope you'll find that special place in your life.

We enjoy your unique—*different*—personalities and talents, but there is a more important "difference" that we hope each of you will embrace. We are hoping and praying that you will come to love Jesus more than anything or anyone else and work hard to be different as he is different. The Bible word for that is "holy." Peter says, "…but as he who called you is holy, you also be holy in all your conduct, since it is written, 'You shall be holy, for I am holy'" (1 Pet 1:15-16).

Four Essential Differences

Let's take a look at four examples of how being different is demonstrated in your everyday life.

First, you will be different because you'll refuse to conform to the world's standards. Paul says, "I appeal to you therefore, brothers, by the mercies of God, to present your bodies as a living sacrifice, holy and acceptable to God, which is your spiritual worship. Do not be conformed to this world, but be transformed by the renewal of your mind, that by testing you may discern what is the will of God, what is good and acceptable and perfect" (Rom 12:1-2).

Think about what it means to "conform" to the world. When we conform to something, we are becoming like that thing. One translation of this verse says, "do not be *poured into the mold* of this world."

When I was 8 and 9 years old, I would go to the Boy's Club in Costa Mesa, California, almost every day. There were a lot of fun things to do there, but I remember pouring Plaster of Paris—a powder that you mix with water—into molds shaped like various animals. When it dried, it hardened into the shape of the mold—the animal—then you painted it and you had a little model of an elephant or lion.

Likewise, if we are "poured into the mold" of the world, we are taking on the shape of the world. What's wrong with that? Just this: when the Bible uses the term "world," it is talking about the common beliefs and values that people in the world tend to adopt. As I write this, the "world" has decided that abortion is "a woman's right to choose"; that homosexuality is OK (and that even two men or two women can be married); that using vile language and using God's name in vain is no big deal; that you can have a relationship with God through any religion; that there is no hell; that God did not create the world, but the world sprung out of nothing by itself; that the Bible is just an old book, nothing special… and on and on.

We are exposed to this kind of anti-biblical teaching every day. If we aren't careful, we will start to believe it because "everyone else does." When that happens, then we have become what Paul warns us against: conformed to the world; and it happens almost before we know it. Now, we are no different than most everyone else and we have drifted far away from God and His word. It's scary. The only antidote is to constantly read God's word—Paul calls it renewing the mind (Rom 12:2).

Conforming to standards is not always wrong, of course. Your school sets standards of behavior and in academics that you must conform to if you want to graduate. There are rules that apply to driving, to sports and to many other areas of life. Jesus intends for us to obey all of the rules that do not contradict what the Bible says.

But if you set your heart on being different than the world—being *holy*—you will not blindly follow the crowd and do what everyone else is doing. You will not adopt the standards of the culture when they conflict with God's word. You will never fall into the trap of "group-think," allowing others to define your view of God, the world, and the Bible. You will be different, in a godly sort of way.

You are all old enough to know by now that it is hard to avoid the pull of this world. The devil wants to "pour you into the mold" of the world and make you just like everyone else. Being different isn't just a "good idea," it is absolutely essential if you want to go to heaven. I can't even bear the thought of not seeing all of you in heaven one day, so I hope you will listen carefully to what God has to say to you about how to get there. It starts by avoiding those things that will mold you into a "worldling."

Second, you'll be different because you will not worry about winning the approval of your friends. This is hard! None of us, at any age, want to be rejected or ignored, and we want people to like us. But if that's our first concern, then we'll begin to compromise our beliefs and put our friends above Christ.

Our family moved a lot because my father (your "Gramps") was a preacher and preachers moved a lot in those days. Several times in my life, I was the new kid in school and new kids were not readily accepted. I hated coming into the classroom in the middle of the semester and I hoped someone—anyone—would be nice to me. I was pretty good in sports, so I used that to gain acceptance from kids who loved sports like I did.

We moved to a new town in the middle of 7th grade and a couple of boys ambushed me, punched me, and made me give them my lunch money. After that, I decided that the best approach was to become friends with them, so I could gain their approval. But they were not the best influence on me. They would go into the local Alpha Beta grocery store and shoplift and tell me to stay outside and watch for the police. That was ridiculous because it was a big store and I didn't know what I was supposed to do if I saw the police, but I did it because I wanted their approval. At the time, at that age, it seemed like it was a matter of life or death. I wanted to be accepted, not hated; who wants to be hated? But they were a bad influence on me and my mom knew it and would quote 1 Corinthians 15:33 ("bad company ruins good morals") every day before I left for school.

Please, don't ever become an "approval addict." Don't become addicted to what other people think about you. For one thing, you'll learn that you can never please everyone; there will always be people who disapprove of you, for one reason or another. But if you seek God's approval, you'll find yourself in the company of others who are seeking God's approval, and they are the kindest, most loving people in the world.

You will be hated by some people—but so what? In John 15:18-25 Jesus tells us not to be surprised when people hate you. He says, "If the world hates you, know that it has hated me before it hated you. If you were of the world, the world would love you as its own; but because you are not of the world, but I chose you out of the world, therefore the world hates you" (John 15:18). He also said, "Woe to you, when all people speak well of you, for so their fathers did to the false prophets" (Luke 6:26).

As I said, this can be really hard—unless we decide to direct our own path and not let others define us. It has always taken courage to be a Christian, and that's still true today. We can do it, though, because Christ will help us. We have to ask God to give us courage and the good sense to follow the words of Christ instead, even when our friends—and perhaps even our *family*—disapprove.

Jesus said, "Do not think that I have come to bring peace to the earth. I have not come to bring peace, but a sword. For I have come to set a man against his father, and a daughter against her mother, and a daughter-in-law against her mother-in-law. And a person's enemies will be those of his own household. Whoever loves father or mother more than me is not worthy of me, and whoever loves son or daughter more than me is not worthy of me" (Matt 10:34-37).

If we value eternal life, then we'll have to put our relationship with Jesus far above all other relationships. You are all fortunate because you have parents and grandparents and cousins who love the Lord and want to stay true to Christ. But even if all of us desert the Lord, you need to say true to him. Jesus says, "No one who puts his hand to the plow and looks back is fit for the kingdom of God" (Luke 9:62).

As I mentioned before, when I was young, my parents quoted 1 Corinthians15:33 ("bad company ruins good morals") to me almost every day, it seemed. I was glad they quoted that a lot because I finally got into my thick skull that I should avoid people who don't want to do the right thing. Most importantly, I decided that I would find someone to marry who shares the same moral and spiritual values. Mimi felt the same way and we found each other. We both agree that we've had a very good life, just trying to follow Jesus instead of others.

Be different. Seek God's direction and shut out all competing voices. It's hard, but with the help of Christ, you can do it.

Third, our moral decisions will show whether or not we are different. 1 Peter 4:1-5 says, "Since therefore Christ suffered in the flesh, arm yourselves with the same way of thinking, for whoever has suffered in the flesh has ceased from sin, so as to live for the rest of the time in the flesh no longer for human passions but for the will of God. For the time that is past suffices for doing what the Gentiles want to do, living in sensuality, passions, drunkenness, orgies, drinking parties, and lawless idolatry. With respect to this they are surprised when you do not join them in the same flood of debauchery, and they malign you; but they will give account to him who is ready to judge the living and the dead."

I've lived long enough to see a radical change in the moral climate, and it causes me to be very concerned about what all of you are facing these days. There is a moral standard that we must adhere to, regardless of what people in the world say. Homosexuality, sexual immorality, immodest dress, cursing, drinking alcohol and watching movies and listening to music and reading with all of this stuff in it is *wrong*.

Our moral decisions will demonstrate whether we are conformed to this world or not.

Our moral decisions are evidence of whether we are seeking the approval of God or of our peers.

Some who do surveys are telling us that the morals of those who claim to be Christians are no different than those of non-Christians. Mimi and I have seen some of the most immodest dresses at "Christian" weddings! My hope for you, Lexi, Kaia and Amyla, is that you will decide *for yourself* and for Jesus' sake that you will wear modest clothing, all the time, because that's what Christians do. Yes, it'll make you different, but that's a good thing because it means you've decided that conforming to Christ is more important than conforming to the world or trying to impress your friends.

Will, Pierce, Reichen and Griffin, we want you to choose, *for yourself* and for Jesus' sake, to do the right thing when it comes to the way you talk, what you listen to and what you watch. There's a lot of garbage on TV and in the movies, as you know. Hollywood is on a mission to make you like the things they decide you should like, to make you over in its image. But that's an ugly image. Violence, sex, and bad language are common in the media, in video games, and in music. Please think about whether you would watch or listen to any of that stuff, or play those games, if Jesus was sitting next to you.

I know your parents are guiding you properly in these things but it's important that you make the proper decisions yourself. Just remember that whatever goes into your brain will stay there forever. Don't do anything today that you'll regret when you get older.

Fourth, you will be branded as "different" because you go to church regularly and believe teachings that are absolutely strange to most people today. This is not new. Listen to this, from 2,000 years ago. Speaking of Paul, Acts 17:19-21 says, "And they took him and brought him to the Areopagus, saying, 'May we know what this new teaching is that you are presenting? For you bring some strange things to our ears. We wish to know therefore what these things mean.' Now all the Athenians and the foreigners who lived there would spend their time in nothing except telling or hearing something new."

Athens is not that much different than any city in the U.S. today. Speak about Jesus today as if he is making a difference in your life, and people are likely to either laugh or look at you like you're weird. And you are, right?

When I was in high school, I was not permitted to go to school dances. When kids would say, "I didn't see you at the dance last night," I would usually say, "Hmmm, I didn't see you either." But, eventually, I would say, "it's against my religion." Those are not very good answers, but the kids would say, "Oh, OK…" Most of the kids went to a church of some kind so, whether they agreed with the rule or not, they understood that if it was "against your religion" you shouldn't do it. It was the same if they said a bad word and then found out my dad was a preacher. "Oh," they would say, "I didn't know your dad was a preacher" and they wouldn't use that language around me anymore.

Also, it was not awkward to mention God and Jesus, or the Bible and church, in those days. In fact, there was a commercial—a public service announcement—that aired every Saturday. It said, "Tomorrow, be sure to attend the church of your choice." Do you believe that? That was on TV!!

Today, mentioning church or the Bible as a reason for doing or not doing something sounds odd to many of your friends. To say, "I believe I should be in church on Sunday so that's where I will be," will be met by, "really?" If you say, "The Bible says…" someone may well say, "you really believe a 2,000 year old book is that important?"

Yes, we can hide our faith, but that won't serve us well when we face God in judgment. To be ashamed of the Bible is to be ashamed of Jesus. That's unacceptable. "So everyone who acknowledges me before men, I also will acknowledge before my Father who is in heaven, but whoever denies me before men, I also will deny before my Father who is in heaven" (Matt 10:32-33).

In summary, if you do these things, you'll be different, alright. But *own* your difference! It takes courage, study, determination and strength, but at the end, you'll find it was all worth it. Mimi and I can tell you, without any hesitation, that choosing to be "different" has made all the difference in the world. We have lived happy, fulfilled lives, with a clear conscience and with confidence that when our life is over, we'll have an eternal home with God in heaven. People may think we're weird, but that's how we're wired because we are wired by God.

And, we have found there is joy in being different. Our hope for you is expressed by Paul in Romans 15:13, "May the God of hope fill you with all joy and peace in believing, so that by the power of the Holy Spirit you may abound in hope."

I love you all!!

Poppy

Questions

1. What is the Bible word for being "different"?

2. Why is it so easy to become conformed to the world's standards and values? What is the only way to avoid being conformed?

3. Why is it dangerous to be over concerning with seeking the approval of others? Did Jesus do that? How did people treat him?

4. Our moral decisions are a good test of whether we are different or not. Give some examples.

5. Why do people find regular attendance at the services of a local church and belief the doctrines taught there so odd today? What is the danger in being ashamed of these things?

7. Stand Firm

Gary Kerr

Dear Carter, Lilly, Molly, Cooper, Sam, Violet, and ???????,

Nani and Pop have had many unforgettable and defining moments in our lives together. But becoming grandparents six times (so far!) is right at the top of the list! We know that you have heard stories about how excited we were to become your grandparents. I immediately nicknamed myself POP, and shouted about it to the world. We fell head-over-heels in love with each of you the moment we met you, and we couldn't wait to begin sharing adventures with you. And that love grows stronger and deeper with each passing day.

What a joy it has been for us to watch you all as you have grown, and to see you develop your own unique personalities. And we hope that you all know how important it is for us to always be here for you, and share with you some valuable lessons that will help you as you go through life.

We wish - perhaps more than you will ever know - that we could promise you a life free from pain, temptation and suffering. But we know all too well from the personal experiences of living life in this world that this will not be true for you. You will face many challenges. As a matter of fact, the Bible tells us that, as Christians, we will be continually engaged in a spiritual battle, that we are at war!

The Apostle Paul tells us (Eph 6:13) to *"take up the whole armor of God, that you may be able to withstand in the evil day, and having done all, to **stand firm**."* In the next few verses, he describes the various pieces of armor that God has given Christians to help them in the battle.

Never underestimate our enemy, Satan. Peter warns us to *"Be sober-minded; be watchful. Your adversary the devil prowls around like a roaring lion, seeking someone to devour"* (1 Pet 5:8). We know that it will be unpleasant and uncomfortable for you all to think about the devil at work in our world. But the Bible frequently speaks about and warns us about him.

Scripture makes it clear that Satan is very real, that he is always working against God and His kingdom, and that he will be working hard to turn you away from God as you grow up. Don't let him win - **STAND FIRM!**

There is a real spiritual war being waged against God, and believers find themselves in this spiritual battle. Our primary concern for you as your grandparents is, "How can we help you to keep from becoming a casualty on the spiritual battlefield?"

This is where Paul's illustration in Ephesians 6 comes in. He uses the Roman soldiers' armor to describe what he calls *"the whole armor of God."* Just as we would protect you, Paul teaches us about the armor of God that we all need for God's protection.

In Ephesians, Paul is writing from prison. Being a prisoner of the Roman Empire, he would have had close interactions with Roman soldiers, and it is the soldier's armor that the apostle uses to show us how God has equipped us with protection from a powerful spiritual enemy. God knows that we are in a spiritual war, and he has given us both armor and weapons for the day of battle. And even though Christ defeated Satan as he was raised from the dead, we still need to be constantly on the alert. Just as an army that has been dealt a decisive blow can still inflict casualties on individual soldiers, Christians can still become casualties of Satan on the spiritual battlefield.

As your grandparents, we so desperately want to help you avoid that awful fate. And God's word tells us that the best way to do that, to **stand firm**, is to *"take up the whole armor of God!"*

Beloved grandchildren, it is only after having put on all the armor of God that you will be fully equipped to **stand firm**. There is so much that can be said about this armor. But for our purpose, Nani and Pop want to share with you some of our thoughts about how this armor can protect you from the schemes of the devil as you grow up and learn how to live as a Christian in a sinful, immoral world.

"Stand therefore, having fastened on the belt of truth!" (Eph 6:14a)

This belt was used by a Roman soldier for two important purposes: To hold the soldier's tunic snugly against his body, to keep it from hindering his movement; and as an accessory on which other things (such as the sword) could be attached. Carter and Cooper, this would be very much like the belts that you wore when you played flag-football. Those belts wrapped around your jerseys, and had some kind of hook on both sides where the flags would be attached.

In the armor of God, the belt is said by Paul to be *"truth,"* and it is found in God's word. In the prayer of Jesus on the night before he was crucified, he said, *"Sanctify them by your truth. Your word is truth."* Culture changes, and worldly values come and go, and Nani and Pop have witnessed incredible cultural changes in our lifetimes. We are very much concerned about how these changes will impact your lives in the future, but we know that if you have the truth of God's word as your foundation; your "centerpiece;" your support; you will be able to **stand firm** against the attacks of Satan. As a Christian, God's word, his *"truth,"* will guide you in a positive way in every area of your life, including how you interact with other people in school, in sports, in business … in everything!

"The breastplate of righteousness!" (Eph 6:14b)

The Roman soldier wore a sleeveless piece of armor that covered his whole upper body, front and back, from neck to waist. It might be made of leather, metal, or chains, and the primary purpose of this heavy armor was to protect his heart and other vital organs. Even though it is not exactly the same, because it doesn't wrap around the whole upper body, think about the chest protector that the umpire wears behind home plate when you have played baseball or softball.

Righteousness is the *"breastplate"* that protects the Christian's heart, and keeps the heart from being wounded and weakened, losing its focus.

Faithfully putting God's truth into practice in our lives, and living righteously, is what it means to put on the *"breastplate of righteousness."* Paul tells us in Philippians 3:9 that our righteousness *"is through faith in Christ, the righteousness which comes from God on the basis of faith."* And so, just as the *"belt"* is closely connected with the truth of God's word, so too is the *"breastplate of righteousness."* We learn how to live righteously by reading, studying, meditating on, believing, and living God's word. To be a Christian and take full advantage of this piece of armor, you will need a thorough knowledge of the Bible ... something we, along with your parents, have been trying to help you achieve since the day you were born.

"As shoes for your feet, having put on the readiness given by the gospel of peace!" (Eph 6:15)

The Roman soldier's shoes were not merely "sandals," but the boots of a warrior, making it possible for him to march confidently into battle. These boots, which at the time were a revolution in warfare, were made with nails through the bottom of the shoe that gripped the ground firmly even when it was slippery, enabling them to travel faster and further than their enemies, and giving them the ability to move quickly over any kind of terrain. Think about all the soccer, baseball, and football shoes that you have worn over the years, with their cleats of various shapes and sizes, to help you get traction on the field. It's the same idea exactly when you think about these Roman soldier's shoes.

When you become a Christian, the gospel gives you peace with God, because your sins have been forgiven and forgotten by God. Similarly, the *"readiness of the gospel of peace"* will equip you to travel over rough roads as you fight against Satan's attacks, and carry this same message of the gospel of peace to others.

"In all circumstances take up the shield of faith, with which you can extinguish all the flaming darts of the evil one!" (Eph 6:16)

The shield referred to here is large, oblong, shaped like a door, and about two to three feet wide and four feet tall. This shield would give protection from the arrows and spears hurled at the Roman soldiers in the heat of battle. Think about the *Lord of the Rings* movies, and remember the scenes where one army unleashed thousands of flaming arrows on the opposing army. And the way they tried to protect themselves was to raise their shields over their heads.

In the same way, we are to use our faith as a shield to protect us from the *"flaming darts of the evil one."* What are those *"flaming darts?"*

In your lives, strong temptations and sinful thoughts will sometimes come upon you suddenly, much like a dart thrown in battle. Satan wants to pierce your defenses and kindle such things as lust, pride, anger, or contempt. When temptations to sin hit their mark, they can set our minds and hearts on fire with wicked thoughts and desires.

What, then, is the *"shield of faith"* that God wants us to use to protect ourselves from these darts? Paul tells us in Romans 10:17, *"So faith comes from hearing, and hearing through the word of Christ!"* Once again, it is the word of God that we use to protect us from Satan's *"flaming darts,"* to shield us from the attacks of Satan. When temptations come, are we going to believe what the devil says, or are we going to believe God and trust in his word?

Our prayer for you, our grandchildren, is that you, like King David, will be protected by God's shield, and can pray like David, *"But you, O LORD, are a shield about me"* (Psa 3:3).

"And take the helmet of salvation!" (Eph 6:17a)

The helmet covered the head and the brain of the soldier, which was, of course the core of a soldier's power to wage war. His ability to think and reason was an important factor in determining his role in victory or defeat. Picture that beautiful *Crimson Tide* football helmet which your beloved Alabama players wear to protect their heads during games, or the metal helmets worn by soldiers in all those *Lord of the Rings* movies. The helmet that protects the mind of the Christian is the knowledge that we are saved.

As Christian soldiers, we must protect our mind and thoughts, focusing them on Christ.

"For to set the mind on the flesh is death, but to set the mind on the Spirit is life and peace." (Rom 8:6)

"Do not be conformed to this world, but be transformed by the renewal of your mind, that by testing you may discern what is the will of God, what is good and acceptable and perfect." (Rom 12:2)

"We destroy arguments and every lofty opinion raised against the knowledge of God, and take every thought captive to obey Christ." (2 Cor 10:5)

The knowledge that we, as Christians, are saved helps us and encourages us to keep our minds and thoughts protected.

"And take ... the sword of the Spirit, which is the word of God!" (Eph 6:17)

The sword of the Roman soldier was a double-edged weapon used for both defense and offense. The sword was used both to protect the soldier when he was being attacked, and to take the attack to the enemy. Maybe the best way to illustrate this is to have you think about all of those *Star Wars* movies that you have seen over and over, with the Jedi Knights using their *Light Sabers.* Sometimes they used the light saber for defense, protecting themselves from attacks of various kinds, and at other times they used them as offensive weapons, pressing the attack against the evil forces of the Galactic Empire. That's exactly how a Roman soldier would have used his sword.

The way you can tell if a person is really a "Christian soldier" is by whether or not, and how, he is using the Word of God. By properly using the scriptures, you can both protect yourself from the enemy, and press the attack and win battle after battle against Satan. The word of God is the one weapon that can assure victory.

"For the word of God is living and active, sharper than any two-edged sword, piercing to the division of soul and of spirit, of joints and marrow, and discerning the thoughts and intentions of the heart." (Heb 4:12)

And this is exactly what we saw Jesus doing when he was tempted by Satan in the wilderness. He deflected the blows of Satan by saying, *"it is written,"* making an appeal to scripture. And he pressed the attack against Satan at the end by once again by saying,

*"Be gone, Satan, for **it is written** ..."* (Matt 4:10).

Please know, however, that the challenge of using any weapon is that it can be dangerous to the one using it if they are not properly trained in its use. Just as Luke Skywalker had to leave his friends and go find Yoda on the planet Dagobah, so that he could practice and learn how to use his weapons, you will need to devote many hours, and much study to the use of God's *"sword,"* so that when the time comes, you will know exactly how to use it both has a means of protection and as a weapon against error and sin.

We plead with you all to start as early as possible reading your bibles, studying God's word, conforming your lives to the truths contained in God's word, and memorizing scripture so that it will be readily available to you when Satan's attacks come. We know that Satan is going to do everything in his power to keep you from spending time in God's word. There are so many distractions in the world, things like movies, and video games, and sports, and TV, and hundreds of others that Satan will use in an attempt to distract you from the really important thing, which is spending time in and learning God's word. "Lay down your sword," he will say, "and spend some relaxing time doing other things!" Don't let him win—**stand firm**!

"Praying at all times in the Spirit, with all prayer and supplication. To that end, keep alert with all perseverance, making supplication for all the saints." (Eph 6:18)

One final tactic - and one that will prove extremely valuable to you in your war against Satan - is prayer! A Christian soldier must pray;

pray in the spirit; pray in a way that is consistent with the sword of the spirit, the word of God.

A Christian soldier will pray at all times, because he recognizes something very important. When we pray we are communicating with "headquarters," and seeking aid and comfort from our "Commander and Chief" himself, the holy, almighty God; the Creator of all things; the God who spoke the universe into existence; the God who made the mountains and the seas; the God who created man from the dust of the earth; the God who parted the Red Sea; the God who sent His Son to deliver us from sin and death. God is eternal, unchanging, all-powerful, all-holy, and sovereign over all things. And we get to communicate with him by being allowed to approach him in prayer!

That's why, our precious grandchildren, it is so important for all of you to learn to be *"praying at all times."* Not just in hard times, when trouble surrounds us and courage fails. We are to be people of prayer in both good times and in bad.

That's why it is so important that we learn *"perseverance"* in prayer. Satan will not rest, and we cannot afford to rest either. Our prayers must be continual and unceasing.

And while you are at it, learn to pray for others as well as for yourself. Pray for your fellow soldiers of the cross all over the world (*"... making supplication for all the saints"*). Pray for your parents. Pray for your cousins who are engaged in the same spiritual conflict that is confronting you. Pray for elders of local churches who are working hard to help equip the saints in their charge to fight and win this spiritual war. And pray for your grandparents, who love you more than life itself, and who want desperately for you to win this war and make it home safely to heaven.

Looking back over what we have written, Nani and Pop fully recognize how inadequate it is, and how much that is important that we have left unsaid. But we fervently hope that reading this will at least give you some awareness and appreciation for how very much we love you all, and how very much we want to be together with all of you - with all our family - in heaven.

Nani and Pop recognize that as Christians, we are in the midst of a spiritual battle, and we thank God that he has equipped us with everything we have needed so far to **stand firm** in the battle with Satan. And we are so thankful that, no matter what happens in this old sinful world, if you, our beloved grandchildren, are also Christians, you also can be well-equipped to successfully face this spiritual battle.

"Finally, be strong in the Lord and in the strength of his might. Put on the whole armor of God, that you may be able to stand against the schemes of the devil!" (Eph 6:10-11)

We love you all SO MUCH, and our prayer for each of you is that you **STAND FIRM** as a good soldier of Jesus Christ!

With all our love ... *always,*

Nani & Pop

Questions

1. According to the apostle Paul in the book of Ephesians, what provision has God made for us as Christians to be able to *"stand against the schemes of the devil?"*

2. Describe in your own words each of the pieces of the Christian's armor:

    a. *"Belt of truth"*
    b. *"Breastplate of righteousness"*
    c. On your feet, shoes that Paul calls *"the readiness given by the gospel of peace"*
    d. *"Shield of faith"*
    e. *"Helmet of salvation"*
    f. *"Sword of the Spirit"*

3. What role does prayer play in our spiritual battle with Satan?

4. Name some people for whom you should be *"praying at all times."*

5. Why is it so important that we prepare ourselves to *"stand firm"* in this life?

8. Learn to be Content

Jon Quinn

To my grandchildren with all my love,

"Do not worry then, saying, "What will we eat?' or "What will we drink?' or "What will we wear for clothing? For the Gentiles eagerly seek all these things; for your heavenly Father knows that you need all these things. But seek first His kingdom and His righteousness, and all these things will be added to you" (Matt 6:31-33).

We were a young family of four at the time we decided to move from a small town in northwest Indiana to work with a small church in Flint, Michigan. Being a small church, we would need others to help support us with the physical necessities of life while we worked with the church, just as the New Testament teaches us to do. I was somewhat intimidated, having two young children who had not even reached school age yet. I would need to "raise support" to be able to make the move. We left what had been our home for four years, and its comforts and security, and travelled to the Birmingham, Alabama area where your grandmother's father, John Barnes, was preaching for a church in Bessemer. We would be staying with your grandmother's parents while I tried to raise the needed support.

But I was worried! I had expenses! We only had a very little saved up. How could I support my family? Our car was not paid off; how could I possibly make the car payments? How could I raise all of the support I needed? I did not sleep well, worrying about pretty much everything. Had I made a mistake? Was my family going to suffer for it?

Things fell into place. But, I am happy to say that I started feeling a lot better about everything not when, but *before* it all worked out. This is important! I said *before* things worked out. As I was praying about it one night, I had been thinking (worrying) about from where the next car payment was going to come. And then, the thought struck me that in the grand scheme of things it did not matter if the car went back to the finance company. There would be some temporary unpleasantness, but nothing compared to the good that could be accomplished if and when we made it to Flint, and we would, *Lord willing*.

I began to get preaching appointments around Birmingham. One preacher was under doctor's orders to let his voice rest, so I filled in for him for a few weeks. Another preacher was moving away and his replacement was not due to arrive for several months and so I filled in there. There were others as well. I was preaching every week and these churches were asking me if they could help support my move to Flint. We moved to Flint in the car that I had been so worried about losing. But even if it had not worked out that way, it would have worked out some way. This life always works out to its best possible conclusion for those who have faith, and whether we kept or lost the car was really a very small, insignificant thing in the grand scheme. For those who trust the King in everything, the King has appointed a Life which never ends. I had under-estimated the graciousness of God and His people. I will need to better remember that next time a crisis must be faced.

Jesus Said Not to Worry

When we read of *"contentment"*, the word that is used in the language in which the New Testament was written is a compound word. This means it is a combination of two words. One word means *"self"* and the other word means *"sufficient"*. Jesus teaches us to *be "self sufficient"*. Self sufficiency depends on being properly equipped by God. It is not learned apart from Him. Our sufficiency is not something found only in ourselves. We must turn to God for it. That is where you will need to go for it.

Self sufficiency is not dependent on outward worldly circumstances. We are not interested in learning how to feel good about a day where everything is going well. Anyone can do that! We want to learn how to feel good about our lives even on days when things do not go very well.

Jesus said to not worry (Matt 6:31-33). He had, just a moment before, asked: *"And who of you by being worried can add a single hour to his life? "* He then concluded, *"So do not worry about tomorrow; for tomorrow will care for itself. Each day has enough trouble of its own"* (Matt 6:27, 34).

To *"worry"* means to be anxious about something. This word comes from a root word which means to be distracted or divided. We ought not to be so filled with worry about things that we are distracted from life's purpose. There needs to be a clear number one priority which becomes our anchor. It needs to be something solid and secure no matter what the day brings. Did you notice what Jesus said this number one priority ought to be? He said that the central thing is seeking first His kingdom and righteousness (notice verse 33 again). We will not allow any worry to distract us from this. Children, let the kingdom be your priority.

In fact, just previous to Jesus' command for us not to worry, He had said, *"No one can serve two masters; for either he will hate the one and love the other, or he will be devoted to one and despise the other. You cannot serve God and wealth"* (Matt 6:24). We cannot serve two masters. If Jesus is our master, then we will not allow ourselves to be distracted from putting His kingdom and righteousness first. So He is not telling us to be unconcerned about our responsibilities. We need to take our responsibilities seriously and the Lord expects us to. This includes grandparents and parents and children. Instead, the point is about not allowing *any* concerns to divide our attention to the point where we are distracted from putting the kingdom first. If we let him, Satan will use those concerns to pull us in his direction. He is really good at using peer pressure to drive a wedge between Jesus and us. He knows that we cannot serve two masters!

Jesus also taught something about the danger of being distracted by worry in His parable of the sower. He describes the hearts of those filled with worry to the point where they become distracted from putting the kingdom first. He says their hearts are like thorny ground. *"And others are the ones on whom seed was sown among the thorns; these are the ones who have heard the word, but the worries of the world, and the deceitfulness of riches, and the desires for other things enter in and choke the word, and it becomes unfruitful"* (Mark 4:18-19).

Worrying is never pleasant. It is something that all want to avoid. Jesus' disciples need to first find their anchor which is putting God's kingdom and righteousness first. This will be a giant step toward becoming content.

Jesus Said Some Things are Less Important Than We Think They Are

One of the keys to finding contentment is not to put too much value on some things while diminishing the value of the truly important. Jesus said, *"Beware, and be on your guard against every form of greed; for not even when one has an abundance does his life consist of his possessions"* (Luke 12:15). Life is more than money and what it can buy. Consider a man who has suffered financial ruin. His business has failed and all he had worked for was gone. He complained, *"I've lost everything"*. With Jesus, a trusting disciple will never have cause to say this. It can never happen. A faithful disciple can suffer loss, but he or she simply cannot lose everything.

No one likes to suffer loss. We grieve over loss. But, still, there is value in sorrow accompanying losses. We are caused to remember things that we never should forget, but sometimes we do. We are reminded of what is really important. In the Old Testament, a wise man wrote about this. He said,

> *It is better to go to a house of mourning*
> *Than to go to a house of feasting,*
> *Because that is the end of every man,*
> *And the living takes it to heart.*
> *Sorrow is better than laughter,*
> *For when a face is sad a heart may be happy.*
> *The mind of the wise is in the house of mourning,*
> *While the mind of fools is in the house of pleasure.* (Eccl 7:2-4)

I have seen this in my life and in others' as well when dealing with a loss. For example, there is a sharp awareness when we experience the death of a loved one that the things we might have been worrying about yesterday were not really very important. The home team losing the ballgame may have upset me yesterday, but today, in the house of mourning, it seems so trivial and silly to have been so worked up over it.

Jesus taught us to choose what is most important. Once He was in the home of His friends in the town of Bethany; Lazarus, Mary and Martha.

Now as they were traveling along, He entered a village; and a woman named Martha welcomed Him into her home. She had a sister called Mary, who was seated at the Lord's feet, listening to His word. But Martha was distracted with all her preparations; and she came up to Him and said, "Lord, do You not care that my sister has left me to do all the serving alone? Then tell her to help me." But the Lord answered and said to her, "Martha, Martha, you are worried and bothered about so many things; but only one thing is necessary, for Mary has chosen the good part, which shall not be taken away from her." (Luke 10:38-42)

It wasn't that Martha was a bad person. She was a good woman. But she sure was frazzled that day! She had many guests to serve. There is nothing wrong with serving guests unless it becomes a distraction from the main thing. It had for Martha. As we have seen earlier, the main thing is putting God's kingdom and righteousness first. Mary had done that. Martha had not. No one would have starved had Martha taken advantage of this very special opportunity presented to her by Jesus' presence in her home.

Learning Process

Paul said that contentment in every situation is something he had to learn. He wrote, *"Not that I speak from want, for I have learned to be content in whatever circumstances I am. I know how to get along with humble means, and I also know how to live in prosperity; in any and every circumstance I have learned the secret of being filled and going hungry, both of having abundance and suffering need"* (Phil 4:11-12). When he learned to put Jesus first, then some of the things that had once been so important to him he no longer worried about. He had found his center. He had an anchor.

Paul had, in Jesus Christ, discovered how to have sufficiency in everything. His contentment had nothing to do with how much or how little he had. He could have much and it not distract him from the kingdom by causing him to be arrogant, prideful or selfish. He could have little without it causing him to be jealous, bitter or resentful. He would always be thankful to God for the things he received, and going without would not crush him or defeat him. To the extent that we are successful at learning what Paul learned, the happier we will be.

We do need to understand that being content does not mean we have no concerns about anything. Paul wrote about his daily concern for all the churches (2 Cor 11:28). He writes of Timothy's *"genuine concern"* for the welfare of the disciples at Philippi (Philippians 2:20). But these are not distracting concerns that take us away from the kingdom and righteousness of God. In fact, they are a part of putting these things first. They do not rob us of our sufficiency.

Jesus Said That We Can Find That For Which We are Searching by Losing Self

Sometimes we find the desirable in unexpected places. Not too long ago, your grandmother was walking to the church building and spotted something shiny in the gravel. She picked it up and discovered that it was a girl's high school class ring. She took it and washed off the dirt and it was found to have a name inscribed. It belonged to one of the members of the congregation. She informed the young lady, now a mother of two, that her ring had been found. It had been missing for over seven years! Years ago the young lady had looked and looked for it at her parents' house because that is where she thought she had lost it. Her whole family had searched for the ring. Of course, they finally gave up. The ring would never have been found at the house, no matter how hard they looked for it, because it wasn't there.

Neither will we find contentment where many people search for it because it is not there. It is someplace else. Remember, we want to find the contentment, or self sufficiency, that stays with us on the bad days as well as the good. We wish to have confidence even during the storms of life and not just on the sunny, pleasant days. So, where do we look for it? Not where most people expect. We will have to look elsewhere.

Jesus said, *"For whoever wishes to save his life will lose it, but whoever loses his life for My sake and the gospel's will save it. For what does it profit a man to gain the whole world, and forfeit his soul? For what will a man give in exchange for his soul?"* (Mark 8:35-37)

We have seen previously that Jesus had said that a (good) life is more than the abundance of possessions we might accumulate. That is where many think they will find the perfect life. But Jesus says I must lose my life to save it. I do not believe He is here referring to physical death when He talks of losing one's life; rather, it is the surrendering of one's life to His kingdom and righteousness. Giving my life to Him is the way to find life, both abundantly and eternally. It is the most profitable and blessed thing I can do. Jesus said that He came so that we could have life abundantly (John 10:10). He makes us sufficient! Understand this! The commandments of Jesus are for our good always (1 John 5:3)!

So, the faithful disciple who has given his or her life to Jesus can never lose everything. But, ironically, the one who refuses to give Jesus his or her life will one day lose everything.

Peace and Strength

Jesus told us not to worry. He made Paul His apostle and sent him into the world to preach His gospel and to build up believers, so it is not surprising that Paul's message would include how not to worry. So, what can I do in a practical way to help me to learn contentment like Paul did? I want to know this secret of sufficiency in every circumstance. I do not want to ruin any of the days of my life with harmful anxiety.

Paul wrote, *"Be anxious for nothing, but in everything by prayer and supplication with thanksgiving let your requests be made known to God. And the peace of God, which surpasses all comprehension, will guard your hearts and your minds in Christ Jesus. Finally, brethren, whatever is true, whatever is honorable, whatever is right, whatever is pure, whatever is lovely, whatever is of good repute, if there is any excellence and if anything worthy of praise, dwell on these things. The things you have learned and received and heard and seen in me, practice these things, and the God of peace will be with you"* (Phil 4:6-9).

Paul says that the antidote to worry includes prayer and supplication with thanksgiving. This means to talk to God about those things which may potentially cause us anxiety. Our hearts and minds will then be guarded by the peace of God which surpasses all comprehension. This causes me to think of that night mentioned earlier as I prayed to God worried about the difficulties our decision to move to Michigan had brought. I remember how surprised I was after praying at how confident and sufficient I was feeling about the situation. What a relief it was! I rejoiced, not in that my circumstance had changed, but my attitude had. I had not expected that. It was beyond my comprehension until it happened. I had prayed about it before, but it was that night that things finally clicked. Everything would be fine no matter which way they turned.

Another occasion when this occurred was when my father, your great grandpa, died. As the funeral approached, people were expressing their condolences. Friends and family visited with one another and we talked about dad. I had thought that this occasion would be full of sorrow almost unbearable. It wasn't. Oh, to be sure, there was sorrow, but it was tempered with joy. We found ourselves smiling and even laughing at dad's quirks, appreciating his love and dedication to God and to us, and in those moments thanking God for the wonderful privilege of having known him. I had not foreseen the joy and peace I experienced that evening, but when it occurred, I was not surprised by it either. I am getting more accustomed to these moments where I find a measure of sufficiency in unexpected places.

Also, notice that Paul concludes by telling us to stay focused on positive things; on things honorable and right and pure and lovely and of good repute. On things that are excellent and worthy of praise is where our minds should dwell. Perhaps we should *"count our blessings; name them one by one."* Someone should write a song about that!

A calm assurance comes to those who trust God. *"And my God will supply all your needs according to His riches in glory in Christ Jesus. Now to our God and Father be the glory forever and ever. Amen."* (Phil 4:19-20). One simply cannot be more sufficient than this. And, with this, comes strength. *"I can do all things through Him who strengthens me"* (Phil 4:13).

I want each of you to learn how to be content. Put His kingdom and righteousness first. Let the truly important things be the most important in your life. Life is so much more than possessions. Let the adequacy found in Christ give you joy, peace and strength in every circumstance. Live life abundantly!

I love you!

To Trent, Elliot, LilyAnne, Persephone, Warner, Timothy, Brooklynn, and Jane Marie

From Grandpa

Questions

1. How does the teaching of Jesus in Matthew 6:31-33 relate to the teaching of Paul in Philippians 4:11-13 regarding contentment?

2. What might be some symptoms of anxiety in our lives that would suggest we need to re-evaluate our kingdom priorities and not be bothered by so many things?

3. What is the value in going to "the house of mourning" (Eccl 7:2-4)? How does doing so help us to remember what is truly important?

4. Compare and contrast Jesus' words to Martha about her anxiety and frustration with His words concerning her sister Mary and her having "chosen the good part" (Luke 10:38-42).

5. Discuss how the instructions found in Philippians 4:6-9 relate to learning contentment (vv. 11-12).

9. Learn to Grow

Leon Mauldin

My Dear Grandchildren,

"I thank my God upon every remembrance of you, always in every prayer of mine making request for you all with joy" (Phil 1:3-4). In Paul's greeting to the Philippians, he did not hide his affection and care: they were on his mind (1:3), in his prayers (1:4), and in his heart (v. 7, "I have you in my heart"). Paul wrote these words to the Philippians, but they express my love and prayers for you, and the joy you have given to your Grandmother (Nunna) and me. We pray to God on your behalf, asking for His blessings on you. We pray that God will protect you from the Evil One, and from the danger of harm from the world. We pray for you to have good health. But there is one thing that is needful (Luke 1:42), and to that end we especially pray, that each of you will go to heaven! That is our overriding concern for you. That you will choose to love the Lord with all of your heart, mind and soul. That you will find your delight in serving Him. "The joy of the Lord is your strength" (Neh 8:10).

I am already so encouraged by what we see up to this point. You all are present each time the church assembles. You read and study God's word at home. You are memorizing scripture, whole chapters. You have made friends of God's children. So I am "confident of this very thing, that He who has begun a good work in you will complete it until the day of Jesus Christ" (Phil 1:6). Already there are so many indications of a good beginning; this is where continued growth on your part will be an essential component.

At the time of this writing, two of you have reached that age of accountability, and have been baptized into Christ (I had the privilege of baptizing you—what a joy!). But as Paul told Timothy, his "true son in the faith" (1 Tim 1:2), "But you must continue in the things which you have learned and been assured of, knowing from whom you have learned them, and that from childhood you have known the Holy Scriptures, which are able to make you wise for salvation through faith which is in Christ Jesus" (2 Tim 3:14-15). Timothy had never had a time when he had not known the Holy Scriptures, having been taught from childhood (infancy, *NIV, NET*) by his mother Lois and grandmother Eunice, then later by the Apostle Paul. But Timothy had made the faith his own. Likewise, you grandchildren have been taught the scriptures literally from infancy. But each of you must make the faith his/her own. What you believe and what you *are* will not be merely because your Mother/Dad believes this, or "the church" teaches that. The "genuine faith" must be in *you* also (2 Tim 1:5). This is truly a growth process, but it must be so. You must make that transition that you individually have a relationship with Jesus that you treasure above all else.

Remember to always thank God for His provisions for our salvation in Christ Jesus. "But He was wounded for our transgressions, He was bruised for our iniquities; The chastisement for our peace was upon Him, And by His stripes we are healed. All we like sheep have gone astray; We have turned, every one, to his own way; And the LORD has laid on Him the iniquity of us all" (Isa 53:5-6). The wages of sin is death (Rom 6:23), eternal separation from God. But Jesus, Eternal Deity, came to earth and became a man, that He might suffer and die for us, that we might be saved. Oh what a difference the Gospel makes! "But thanks be to God, that, whereas ye were servants of sin, ye became obedient from the heart to that form of teaching whereunto ye were delivered; and being made free from sin, ye became servants of righteousness" (Rom 6:17-18, *ASV*).

But not only do we need the blood of Jesus to save us from every past sin, which takes place at the point of baptism; we continue to need the cleansing blood of Jesus. When Paul said, "for all have sinned and fall short of the glory of God" (Rom 3:23), he not only meant that all have sinned in the past, but that all *continue* to fall short. John wrote, "But if we walk in the light as He is in the light, we have fellowship with one another, and the blood of Jesus Christ His Son cleanses us from all sin. If we say that we have no sin, we deceive ourselves, and the truth is not in us. If we confess our sins, He is faithful and just to forgive us our sins and to cleanse us from all unrighteousness" (1 John 1:7-9).

I write these things, not to discourage you, but to help you deal with life's realities. Your Granddaddy is not perfect (far from it). You are not perfect. You will make mistakes. What you do when you realize you have failed is important. On such occasions, Satan, our enemy, would have you believe that there is no use trying to serve the Lord, that you may as well quit trying. Satan has many devices (2 Cor 2:11). One of his greatest weapons is discouragement. Please resolve never to quit because of failure or for any other reason! "My little children, these things I write to you, so that you may not sin. And if anyone sins, we have an Advocate with the Father, Jesus Christ the righteous. And He Himself is the propitiation for our sins, and not for ours only but also for the whole world" (1 John 2:1-2).

Our Heavenly Father loves us so much. "For as the heavens are high above the earth, So great is His mercy toward those who fear Him; As far as the east is from the west, So far has He removed our transgressions from us. As a father pities his children, So the LORD pities those who fear Him . . . But the mercy of the LORD is from everlasting to everlasting On those who fear Him, And His righteousness to children's children, To such as keep His covenant, And to those who remember His commandments to do them" (Psa 103:11-13, 17-18). It is essential then to make it your consistent practice, that whenever sin occurs, to repent of it, acknowledge it before God, and pray for His forgiveness. Then put it behind you, except to learn from it, and determine not to continue in it.

While on this topic of determining to learn from failures, remember that Jesus wants us not only to cease from doing wrong but to have a resolute commitment to do what is right. Jesus used the illustration of the man who had a demon cast out, but the "house" (the man himself; his heart) remained "empty (unoccupied, NIV), swept, and put in order." In that case the demon found seven more demons and they all made their home in that man (Matt 12:43-45). It's not enough to stop doing that which is sinful; you must fill your heart with good things, like those listed in Philippians 4:8: "Finally, brethren, whatever things are true, whatever things are noble, whatever things are just, whatever things are pure, whatever things are lovely, whatever things are of good report, if there is any virtue and if there is anything praiseworthy -- meditate on these things."

My Dear Grandchildren, God wants you to grow in grace and knowledge of our Lord and Savior Jesus Christ (2 Pet 3:18). So many get off to a good start as they obey the conditions of Gospel obedience, but then seem to have no compass, no sense of direction afterward. This is so sad, because God has a plan for us. Once we become His children He wants us to continue to grow for the rest of our lives! Jesus said, "A disciple is not above his teacher, but everyone who is perfectly trained will be like his teacher" (Luke 6:40). A disciple is a pupil (NASB); he is a student (NIV). Think of it this way—for the rest of your life you will be "in school," as you continue the *training* process, to be *like your Teacher* (Jesus). Do you see how this calls for your learning to grow?

For example, when you see how Jesus was compassionate, you will want to become compassionate also. His compassion was extended to those who had special needs, such as those who were sick or had lost loved ones; you also are learning to weep with those who weep. But Jesus was compassionate toward those who were lost; you will likewise want to grow in your desire to teach others the Gospel that they might be saved from their sins. So it is will all of the wonderful traits of Jesus. You will want to grow into His likeness.

Paul said, "that we should no longer be children, tossed to and fro and carried about with every wind of doctrine, by the trickery of men, in the cunning craftiness of deceitful plotting, but, speaking the truth in love, may grow up in all things into Him who is the head—Christ" (Eph 4:14-15). There is a sense in which you must always be *childlike* (humble, teachable, submissive), but you are to grow and mature, because the winds of false doctrine are always blowing. You must grow up into *what?* Our text answers, "Into Christ." So many passages show us that this is God's plan for us;

that we learn to grow into being more and more like Jesus. "Conformed to the image of His Son" (Rom 8:28). "But we all, with unveiled face, beholding as in a mirror the glory of the Lord, are being transformed into the same image from glory to glory, just as by the Spirit of the Lord" (2 Cor 3:18). "Christ in you, the hope of glory."

What does all of this mean to you? It requires first that you must learn to have a certain kind of mind. "If then you were raised with Christ, seek those things which are above, where Christ is, sitting at the right hand of God. Set your mind on things above, not on things on the earth. For you died, and your life is hidden with Christ in God. When Christ who is our life appears, then you also will appear with Him in glory" (Col 3:1-4). Dear Children, I pray for you to have this kind of spiritual mindset!

Further, "I beseech you therefore, brethren, by the mercies of God, that you present your bodies a living sacrifice, holy, acceptable to God, which is your reasonable service. And do not be conformed to this world, but be transformed by the renewing of your mind, that you may prove what is that good and acceptable and perfect will of God" (Rom. 12:1-2). When you arise from the watery grave of baptism, you are a babe in Christ. But you must understand that you have made a commitment to become this living sacrifice unto God. There will always be peer pressure, not just when you are young. Don't let the world squeeze you into its mold. Instead be transformed (remember we've studied that word "metamorphosis," a change of form, like the caterpillar to the butterfly) by the renewing of your mind. Remember that you "prove" the will of God as you put it to the test by living it, by doing it.

How can you keep on growing? Do you remember that the Hebrew Christians had stopped growing, they had lost their joy in serving the Lord, they had grown weary? They needed someone to teach them again even the first principle of the Gospel (Heb 5:11-14). What could be done to help them recover and start growing again? The answer, found throughout the book of Hebrews, is to recapture and then to keep their focus on Jesus! Consider these verses: "But we see Jesus" (2:9); "Consider the Apostle and High Priest ... Jesus Christ" (3:1; 4:14-16; 7:25). "But we have such a High Priest" (8:1); "Looking unto Jesus" (12:2); "For consider Him" (12:3). I mention these verses because not only will they help a struggling Christian recover, but keeping your focus on Jesus will help *prevent* your stumbling, and will insure your steady and continued growth.

Another essential in your growth in the Lord is to learn to hate evil. "Let love be without hypocrisy. Abhor what is evil. Cling to what is good" (Rom 12:9). That which is evil and sinful will hinder your growth: "Therefore, laying aside all malice, all deceit, hypocrisy, envy, and all evil speaking, as newborn babes, desire the pure milk of the word, that you may grow thereby, if indeed you have tasted that the Lord is gracious" (1 Pet 2:1-3). The sinful things listed here should be avoided first because they are sinful; God says not to do these things. But you are learning to look at a passage in its context. If you are to grow by taking in the pure milk of the word, you must put off anything that would hinder your walk with God. Note that in this list many of these sins are on the "inside" and may be harder to see than some other sins, like drunkenness or murder. But all of these sins would make you impure and would prevent your growth in the Lord. Take sin seriously! "Therefore, having these promises, beloved, let us cleanse ourselves from all filthiness of the flesh and spirit, perfecting holiness in the fear of God" (2 Cor 7:1).

You've heard Granddaddy say that the Great Commission has two parts. "Go therefore and make disciples of all the nations, baptizing them in the name of the Father and of the Son and of the Holy Spirit, teaching them to observe all things that I have commanded you" (Matt 28:19-20). Part 1 is when the Gospel is taught, when one believes, repents, and is baptized into Christ for the remission of sins. How long does that take? For some it was the "same hour of the night" (Acts 16:33). For many in the book of Acts it was the first time they heard a Gospel sermon. But then there is Part 2, "teaching them [those taught & baptized] to observe all things that I have commanded you." How long does that take? That, Dear Grandchildren, is to define the rest of your life. Continuing to learn, always with a view to obeying, what Jesus has said!

"But also for this very reason, giving all diligence, add to your faith virtue, to virtue knowledge, to knowledge self-control, to self-control perseverance, to perseverance godliness, to godliness brotherly kindness, and to brotherly kindness love. For if these things are yours and abound, you will be neither barren nor unfruitful in the knowledge of our Lord Jesus Christ" (2 Pet 1:5-8). Peter goes on to describe what I so much want for each of you: "for so an entrance will be supplied to you abundantly into the everlasting kingdom of our Lord and Savior Jesus Christ" (2 Pet 1:11).

Dear Grandchildren, the Bible says of Jacob and his youngest son Benjamin, "his life is bound up in the lad's life" (Gen 44:30). Your Nunna & I feel that way toward you; our lives are bound up in your lives; we are inseparably connected with you; we love you with all our hearts! We regard you each as wonderful blessings from God (Prov 17:6; Psa 128:1-6). Will, you will always be our special firstborn. Noel (note that is *Leon* spelled backwards, BTW), I've never seen a girl more like her mother. Samuel, you were born with a smile, and you are a source of joy to us. Leon, I'm glad we share the same name; you are greatly loved. Rinoa, what a joy you are. Keegan, you continue to amaze us and amuse us. Our special Owen, you are never forgotten, you are in our hearts forever; we know you are safe in the arms of Jesus. And last but not least, Celes Maria (now just a few weeks old); we anticipate great joy from you!

Questions

1. Why is it important to make the faith your own, as Timothy did? (2 Tim. 1:5)

2. What should you do when you realize you have failed, and how is the proper response essential to continued growth?

3. Discuss how growth means not only abstaining from that which is sinful but also "filling the house" with good things.

4. What does the term "disciple" as used by Jesus in Luke 6:40 tell us about growth?

5. Explain what is meant by the Great Commission having two parts.

> **Who Will Be the Influence?**
>
> *If young people have just a few adults who will come alongside them and encourage them to grow in their faith, there's a much better chance they will remain in the church and be rooted in Jesus long into adulthood. So one or two positive influences can make a world of difference in the faith — and life — of a young person.*
>
> McFarland, Alex; Jimenez, Jason. *Abandoned Faith: Why Millennials Are Walking Away and How You Can Lead Them Home.* Kindle Edition, Locations 896-899.

10. Learn to Forgive

Jim Deason

My Dearest Grandchildren,

As I sit in front of my computer to write this letter my mind floods with so many memories it is hard to concentrate long enough to compose. My eyes are blurred with tears as I remember your laughter and occasionally your pain. Eighteen years ago I was away from home, preaching in Eastern Kentucky, when the news came that Hannah was about to be born. Time stood still until I learned that both mother and baby were fine. So bad did I want to be there that I could hardly finish preaching the meeting. To say the least, I was excited. Tomorrow will be Nora's second birthday. Oh, sweet Nora, how heart-warming is your smile? You wear the number "10" at Camp Mamaw and Grandpaw. Each of you know, from one to ten, that you have a special place in my heart that none other could ever occupy. You have filled my life with more joy than I can possibly explain.

Other men have written in this book of lessons they want their grandchildren to learn. Please read them—each one of them—for they are written by men seasoned with years of experience. They have their own grandchildren in mind, as do I, but you can learn much from what they write. Hear the words of the wise.

If I could ask of God one special gift it would be the ability to help all men see the enormity of their sin and the tragedy of its consequences. Why? It breaks my heart to even think this, but I know you are going to sin (Rom. 3:23). I want you to be able to recognize your sin, what it does to the heart of God, what it does to your relationship with Him, and the danger it poses to your eternal destiny. Sin puts you at enmity with God and in danger of losing your soul. Nothing, NOTHING, is worse than sin.

The wise man understood this and he warned, "Do not enter the path of the wicked and do not proceed in the way of evil men. Avoid it, do not pass by it; Turn away from it and pass on" (Prov 4:14-15). Why? Because he knew what all must learn, that the end of sins way is death (Prov. 14:12; cf. Rom 6:23). The good news is that forgiveness can be found in the soul-cleansing blood of Jesus. "You (are) not redeemed with perishable things... but with the precious blood, as of a lamb unblemished and spotless, the blood of Christ" (1 Pet 1:18-19).

Forgiveness is an attribute of God that moves Him to treat you, a sinner, as though your sin was never committed. Forgiveness removes the enmity your sin puts between you and God, releases you from the spiritual consequences of your sin, and restores your relationship with Him. This the reason the Ethiopian nobleman "went on his way rejoicing" after being baptized for the forgiveness of his sins (Acts 2:38; 8:38-39). He was happy man. Forgiveness is something to be happy about.

Some of you, my beloved grandchildren, have already obeyed the gospel. I am so proud of you. I have every reason to believe that as the rest of you age and mature you'll follow suit and give your lives to Jesus. It is the best and most important decision you will ever make in life. I rejoice to see the day.

I have said all of this to lay a foundation for what I really want to write to you about.

The problem of sin reaches beyond your relationship with God. If God grants you to live long enough, there will be times when you will sin against other people and other people will sin against you. When this happens someone is going to get hurt. Sometimes bitter feelings ensue and a relationship is threatened, if not destroyed. There are some who sin against one another who have hearts filled with hate and harsh grudges are sometimes held for many years. I have preached the gospel for forty-five years and more. I've seen churches crippled by these attitudes, rendered impotent to work together in the kingdom of God. Sometimes these bitter feelings have spilled out into the community giving occasion for the enemies of the Lord to blaspheme and causing others to stumble at the preaching of truth. This is a shame—a disgrace—that it happens among the people of God, but it does. I *never* want it to happen to you.

People need to learn to forgive one another. When we are able to forgive, love reigns supreme and we can experience "the unity of the Spirit in the bond of peace" (Eph 4:3). In a church where people practice forgiveness, men, women, and children can grow spiritually and their prayers can ascend to the throne of God unhindered. Peter commanded that "all of you be harmonious, sympathetic, brotherly, (and) kindhearted…" (1 Pet 3:8) but that can't happen unless we learn to forgive others when they wrong us.

You've spent a lot of time at Mamaw and Grandpaw's house. We have often closed our day by singing together the songs you loved as you grew up. At our house, "Jesus Loves Me" has been more than a song set to a tune, it was a message we wanted to indelibly imprint upon your hearts. We have opened our Bible to talk about the story of God creating the world, Noah and the Flood, and David and Goliath. We have talked about the cross. Bible study between us is nothing new. It is as natural to us as breathing. So, here we go again. Let's talk about the importance and necessity of forgiving one another. Let's talk about how to learn to forgive.

The first thing I want to say to you is that *the Bible actually commands us to forgive*. Paul said, "So, as those who have been chosen of God, holy and beloved, put on a heart of compassion, kindness, humility, gentleness and patience; bearing with one another, and *forgiving each other*, whoever has a complaint against anyone; *just as the Lord forgave you, so also should you*" (Col 3:12–13; cf. 1 Cor 14:37). We call Jesus "the blessed and only Sovereign, the King of kings and Lord of lords" (1 Tim 6:15), and so He is. That being true, our responsibility is to subject ourselves to His rule (Matt 28:18) in unquestioned obedience. There are no nonessential commands of God. As sure as we are commanded to believe (Acts 16:31), repent, and be baptized (Acts 2:38), we are also commanded to forgive. You have heard it said, "Either Jesus is Lord of ALL, or He is not Lord at all!" It's simple, just do it because Jesus said it!

Forgiveness, however, is more than a command. Knowing how hard it is to forgive those who hurt us *Jesus demonstrated it for us*. Can you imagine His anguish at being rejected by those He created? Imagine the agony of the scourging He endured, and the pain of the nails that held Him to the cross. Still, as He breathed life's last few breaths he prayed, "Father, *forgive them*; for they do not know what they are doing" (Luke 23:34). Has anyone ever treated you so despicably? I don't think so. If Jesus could pray for the forgiveness of those who crucified Him, I think you have the ability to forgive those who sin against you.

You might be thinking, "Yes, Jesus forgave those who crucified Him, BUT He was the Son of God. How can I be expected to forgive like He did?" I want you to know that, when Jesus came to earth, He assumed the human condition with all its frailties, aches, and pains (Phil 2:7-8; Heb 2:14) and was made a perfect high priest able to "sympathize with our weaknesses... tempted in all things as we are, yet without sin" (Heb 4:15). Jesus knows. He endured and you can also. He is your example (1 Pet 2:21-22) and you need to have confidence in Him.

If there is a lingering doubt in your mind about your ability to forgive *think about Mary, the mother of Jesus*, and the early church. I cannot think of anything more agonizing than to stand by a cross watching my son die, but she did (John 19:25). Afterward, she remained in Jerusalem and was present when the disciple assembled in the upper room (Acts 1:14). Though we are not told specifically, it is but a small assumption to think she remained in Jerusalem and was present on Pentecost. If that is the case she saw people, assembled to hear Peter, who had crucified her son (Acts 2:22-23). She witnessed as some of these same people received the word and were baptized (Acts 2:41). Now consider, "All those who had believed were *together*... Day by day continuing *with one mind* in the temple, and breaking bread from house to house, *they were taking their meals together* with gladness and sincerity of heart" (Acts 2:44,46). Is it possible that she broke bread with some of the very people who crucified her son? It sure looks like it to me. *That is forgiveness!*

How is it possible that these people could forgive so much wrong others had committed against them? I think there are several answers, actually. *First, there is the matter of love.* Jesus said to His disciples, "A new commandment I give to you, that you love one another, even as I have loved you, that you also love one another" (John 13:34). Love has many characteristics. It is patient, kind, and humble. It is not self-centered, not easy to retaliate, and doesn't keep a running record of all the things others have done to you. Love is able to see the best in people, hope for the best, and helps you to endure when things don't go just the way you think they should. Love is never going to let you down (cf. 1 Cor 13:4-7). I realize that forgiveness is not specifically mentioned in this list, but it sure seems to me that it is imprinted in every letter. If you love in this fashion, if you love the way Jesus loved you, the motivation to forgive others when they hurt you is within you.

Second, there is the "golden rule." In His famous *Sermon on the Mount* Jesus commanded, "In everything, therefore, treat people in the same way you want them to treat you" (Matt 7:12). I call this the "Cardinal Relationship Principle" because no relationship can survive very long and prosper without it. It is simple, really. Do you know how you like to be treated? Treat other people in the same way. Do you want other people to forgive you when you sin against them? Then forgive them when they sin against you. This principle is *simple*. Everyone of mature mind can understand and obey it. This rule is *inclusive*. There is no situation omitted. This principle applies everywhere, with everyone, in every relationship, and in every circumstance. This rule is *conclusive*. Jesus said, "do it," (see esp., KJV, ASV, ESV). The "golden rule" is not an option, it is a mandatory code of conduct. This principle demands that, if you want others to forgive you, then forgive them!

Third, the concept of reciprocal forgiveness is taught in a number of places in the Bible, and from another angle. Think about Paul's statement in Ephesians 4:32: "Be kind to one another, tenderhearted, forgiving each other, just as God in Christ also has forgiven you." God is saying that you are to forgive others because He has forgiven you. Jesus paid sin's price at Calvary. "But God demonstrates His own love toward us, in that while we were yet sinners, Christ died for us. Much more then, having now been justified by His blood, we shall be saved from the wrath of God through Him (Rom 5:8–9). I remind you that this is the price God paid for *your sins*, a demonstration of His love for *you*. If God so loved you that He gave His Son to die for you—forgiving you—then, let this be your motivation to forgive others. Do not dare to let bitter grudges keep you out of heaven! Release it! Let it go!

That's looking to the past in a sense—forgive others as God has forgiven you—finding motivation in what has already happened. Now let's look forward. Do you understand that sin is not only in your past, but in your future, too? I know you do not plan to sin—your heart is too pure and innocent to scheme wickedness—but, if you live long enough, Satan will invade your heart and you will sin against God again. The history of man is too clear to deny the future (Rom 3:23). If you want God's forgiveness the next time you sin, then forgive others who have sinned against you. "If you forgive others for their transgressions, your heavenly Father will also will forgive you" (Matt 6:14). Your own forgiveness by God is conditioned upon you forgiving others. "Blessed are the merciful, for they shall receive mercy" (Matt 5:8).

I love the conversations we share. I love to listen when you are happy. I hurt when you tell me you are hurting and why.

"Grandpaw, how do I do what Jesus wants me to do? How do I forgive this person who has hurt me so?" Because of my own failings I understand the difficulty. It is easy to tell you to forgive, it is easy to point you to the Biblical motivation to forgive, but the "rubber meets to road" when we face the question of "How?". There are, I believe, some concrete steps you can to help you walk the path of forgiveness.

1) Confront the one who hurt you (Matt 18:15-17). If you truly love someone and desire their salvation, you will act out of love and seek their repentance. If they repent, forgive them. If they do not repent, then act accordingly and follow through with what the Scripture enjoins.

2) Pray for the one who sinned against you by name. Trust me, I've been there. It's hard to feel unforgiving and hold a grudge when you are calling someone's name in prayer as you go before the throne of God. Jesus said, "pray for those who persecute you" (Matt 5:44). Follow both His example (Luke 23:34), and that of Stephen (Acts 7:60). If they could pray for their enemies, you can also.

3) Remember, harboring unforgiveness in your heart does far more harm to you than it does to the person who has wronged you. They likely put their wrong behind them, not giving it hardly more than a moments notice, and moved on quickly. What they did to you is in their rear view mirror and your feelings and attitudes are left in the wake of the disaster they caused. Do not let bitterness and dwelling on past wrongs define who you are today. You are better than that!

4) You will find it easier to forgive when you reflect on how much

you have been forgiven. Candidly examine yourself (2 Cor 12:5). You can use your failures as a springboard to forgive others.

5) Search for the good in the person who has done you wrong. Sometimes we get tunnel vision when looking at those who hurt us. Their wrong is all we see and, in our mind, we let their one action define how we view them. That is not fair and we wouldn't want others do that to us (remember the "golden rule"). I'm not saying that you should overlook their sin, we shouldn't. I am saying that it is helpful in forgiving others if you can broaden the context and see the good they otherwise do.

6) Try to understand the person who hurt you. There is usually a reason why people act the way they do. They may be a victim of their own heredity or environment; or, they may have had something misrepresented to them, resulting in their offensive behavior. Understanding them doesn't change the fact that you need to confront the offender, but it could change your method of approach. Sometimes it is impossible to understand why people act as they do, but when you can it is helpful.

I know there is more to be said about learning to forgive, but I hope these few words will help you as you navigate the challenges of life.

Dearest Hannah, Emily, Julia, Emma, Jay, Joshua, Caleb, Isaac, Liam, and Nora. I pray for you life's greatest blessings. I never want harm or pain to befall you, nor anyone to hurt you, but I can't protect you from it all, nor should I. Trials produce perseverance, perseverance produces proven character, and proven character produces a hope that will not disappoint (Rom. 5:3-5).

To use a football analogy, your Mamaw and I are in the fourth quarter of life. There's a lot more of it behind us than ahead. We are in pretty good health, but we are already beginning to feel our bodies wearing down. Yet, we want you to know that our "inner man is being renewed day by day" because we are looking for the eternal (2 Cor 4:16-5:1). Our eyes are fixed "on Jesus, the author and perfecter of faith" (Heb 12:2) like never before, and our hope is steadfastly anchored in Him.

We want you, too, to be anchored in Jesus and to have this same hope the two of us share. There will be people who will hurt you, but through it all you will grow into the strong Christians God wants you to be. You know how I love for us all to be together. What a joy it will be to gather around the throne of God with you one day. May God help us all to that end.

Your loving Grandpaw

Questions

1. After reading Proverbs 4:14-15 and Matthew 5:29-30, discuss what steps you should take to avoid sin.

2. In your own words, what does forgiveness mean? What does forgiveness look like to you?

3. What are some important ways in which forgiveness adds to the unity of the local church?

4. What is the connection between love and forgiveness?

5. Discuss forgiveness and the "golden rule." Can you give an example?

6. Be prepared to discuss the six steps to learning to forgive? Can you add to this list?

Purpose in Life

The purpose of life is to bring honor to God, to know, love, and obey Him, to become like Him, and to live for His purposes in this world as I prepare to live in the next one. A life that is intentionally lived for this purpose will be characterized by certain attitudes and actions. For one thing, if I am to progress in this sort of life, I must regularly live for a larger whole. I must live for the kingdom of God and be involved aggressively in the war between that kingdom and the kingdom of darkness.

Moreland, J. P.. *Love Your God with All Your Mind: The Role of Reason in the Life of the Soul.* Navpress, Kindle Edition, Locations 1476-1480).

11. Control Your Emotions

Warren E. Berkley

Dear Grandchildren,

In conversations we've had and in the teaching and preaching you've been privileged to hear, you've heard the truth that God made you. The Bible says that He made you "in His image," (Gen. 1:27). This is not said about rocks, trees or animals. God made human beings in His image.

This doesn't mean you look like God in physical appearance, or that you can do supernatural things like God can do. Think beyond visual similarity and the supernatural acts. It means there are certain characteristics of God that He put in you.

God is capable of thought, reasoning and memory. You have those capacities. God can communicate, so can you. God can listen, so can you. That's the way this works. You were made in God's image and that means in certain ways you reflect the personal traits of your Creator.

I'm asking you to consider the part of you that feels. Emotions. When you get angry, that is an emotion. When you are happy, laughing, maybe jumping up and down, that is an emotion. When you feel something inside—love or hate—that is an emotion. You have emotional capacity because God made you in His image.

There are traits you have that God put in human beings, and one of those is your emotional capacity (feelings).

Like everything else God has given to you, you must take responsibility and learn discipline (self-control) over your emotions. God expects this of you. Jesus Christ, who lived and died for you, has provided both example and instruction to enable you to be emotionally mature. That is, to keep your emotions well placed in your life.

The Bible gives us examples of people with emotions out of control. One of the first examples is Cain, the son of Adam and Eve and the brother of Abel. The story is told in Genesis chapter four. Both Cain and Abel worshipped God. Abel's worship was acceptable to God. Cain's worship was not. Cain became very emotional – angry! That emotion led him to murder his brother. Here is an example of emotion out of control, not restrained. God said to Cain, "you must rule over it" (Gen 4:7). That means, Cain should have controlled his anger and not let the sin occur. God is showing us, in this story, that emotions can get out of control, hurt others and ruin us. Beyond that, God is not pleased when we let emotions rule us and take us away from Him.

You have heard me and others warn you of something called "emotional immaturity." By that I mean relying on the feelings of the moment, rather than good values. God gave you and me the capacity to feel, to love, to desire, even to become agitated. But He expects us to control how we feel. If you don't learn emotional maturity now, in your youth, it may become a real problem in your adult life when you must interact with other adults, maintain good relationships, hold a job and be a productive citizen and church member.

Here's what will help you more than anything. What Jesus did and what Jesus said.

Jesus is our perfect example of emotional maturity. If anyone who has ever lived on earth had a "reason" to blow up with emotional impulse, Jesus did – when you consider how He was treated. But though He was firm about serving God and telling people about the ruin of sin, He is a perfect example of self-control. He was angry with people rebelling against God, but did not ever exhibit a regrettable outburst (see Matt 21:12-13; Mark 11:15-18; John 2:13-22; Eph 4:26). Jesus spoke the truth in love, took decisive action for the good of people, but always exhibited control of His emotions. His anger had proper motivation and targeted sinful behavior and injustice. He grieved, rejoiced and was tempted (see Matt 4:1-11), but never allowed His emotional side to find unwise or hurtful expression. Loyalty to God was His priority. His example reflects that.

We observe in the life of Jesus, the full range of legitimate human emotions, yet never any sin or compromise. He wept at the grave of Lazarus (John 11:33-36); He wept as He approached Jerusalem (Luke 19:41-44); He showed tenderness in the presence of little children (Mark 10:13-16); He was angered by the hardened hearts of sinners (Mark 3:5); and He showed emotions when driving out the money changers from the temple (John 2:13-16). Jesus is our example of emotional expression but without any ugly impulse or absence of discipline. He kept His emotions in check.

Jesus gave instruction that you can apply to be emotionally mature. He sent apostles to reveal His will, that we have written in the New Testament. Those writings are rich with simple instruction from Jesus for us to learn emotional maturity. For example, in James 1:19-20. "…let every person be quick to hear, slow to speak, slow to anger, for the anger of man does not produce the righteousness of God." Sometimes we need to slow down and that helps us control emotional outbursts (Prov 19:11; 29:22; 14:29; 16:32). It may be very difficult. But again, learning this control early will serve us well later in life. And, this discipline is pleasing to God, who made us in His image. When I was a little boy, I heard adults say, "count to ten." When agitated or upset with someone, before reacting or speaking – the idea was to "count to ten." That simply meant, slow down before you explode. Don't act on impulse and get into trouble. "The less you control your emotions, the greater the risk of destroying important relationships," (*The Teenage Brain*, by Frances E. Jensen with Amy Ellis Nutt).

Remember that how you respond to being wronged is part of what defines your character. "Repay no one evil for evil, but give thought to do what is honorable in the sight of all" (Rom 12:17).

You have a responsibility to contribute to the peace that is so important in your family. Outbursts not only display immaturity and displease God, such impulses cause great stress and destroy peace in your family. Author Erma Bombeck once said: "When my kids become wild and unruly, I use a nice, safe playpen. When they're finished, I climb out." That's funny but it helps us see what stress we can cause for people we love.

Quick emotional outbursts are damaging, as illustrated by this interesting story.

Nails In The Fence
Author Unknown

There once was a little boy who had a bad temper. His father gave him a bag of nails and told him that every time he lost his temper, he must hammer a nail into the back of the fence.

The first day the boy had driven 37 nails into the fence. Over the next few weeks, as he learned to control his anger, the number of nails hammered daily gradually dwindled down. He discovered it was easier to hold his temper than to drive those nails into the fence.

Finally the day came when the boy didn't lose his temper at all. He told his father about it and the father suggested that the boy now pull out one nail for each day that he was able to hold his temper. The days passed and the young boy was finally able to tell his father that all the nails were gone.

The father took his son by the hand and led him to the fence. He said, "You have done well, my son, but look at the holes in the fence. The fence will never be the same. When you say things in anger, they leave a scar just like this one. You can put a knife in a man and draw it out. It won't matter how many times you say I'm sorry, the wound is still there."

The little boy then understood how powerful his words were.

He looked up at his father and said "I hope you can forgive me father for the holes I put in you."

"Of course I can," said the father.
http://www.inspirationpeak.com

But emotions are not limited to anger. I'm certain you will hear people say something like, "whatever you feel like doing, go ahead," or "if it feels right, it must be OK." **IF IT FEELS GOOD, DO IT?** First, the Bible never says anything like this. When you hear these statements, please remember, they didn't come from God. God expects us to control ourselves and devote our minds and bodies to Him (Romans 12:1,2).

In the time of your youth, an attraction can develop toward a person. As you spend time with this person and enjoy their company, temptation can create emotions that need to be checked very carefully. Boy and girl relationships and dating is often a challenge to our emotional side. You may need to have a conversation with a parent or grandparent, to discuss those feelings and receive advice. In the heat of romance, emotions can lead you to some serious mistakes. Remember Christ's example and teaching. Let more experienced people help you. While God gave you the capacity for feelings, He expects you to let His will govern how you use those feelings. **In fact, everything God gives you comes with the responsibility to use those gifts to serve Him (Rom 12:3-8; 1 Pet 4:11; Psa 100:3).**

If you live your life driven primarily by selfish emotions (anger, ambition, appetite), not only does this way of life take you away from God, it subjects you to a variety of risky behaviors. And, emotion-driven living tends to reject good counsel from wise people in your life. " — a jacked- up, stimulus- seeking brain not yet fully capable of making mature decisions — hits teens pretty hard, and the consequences to them, and their families, can sometimes be catastrophic." (*The Teenage Brain*, by Frances E. Jensen with Amy Ellis Nutt).

Consider also the impact of your influence on others. If your emotional discipline is obviously lacking, how will you exert a good influence on others? Even if you tell people you are a Christian and you relate to them some of the teaching of Christ – if your actions are not in harmony with the teachings of Christ, your influence will not lead your friends in the right direction. Following Jesus includes taking others to Christ. Absence of self-control will work against that high purpose.

Likewise, in religion, you will hear a lot about emotions. For many religious people, it is more about emotional display than obedience to God. There are people with enthusiasm or passion, but they are not submitting to God's will (Rom 10:1-3). Emotion in our relationship with God is legitimate and encouraged, but it is a result not a cause. When the man from Ethiopia became a Christian, he went on his way rejoicing (see Acts 8:39). Joy was a result of what? His obedience to God, having received the forgiveness of his sins. I want you to remember, while emotions are a part of your relationship with God – the basis of your relationship with God is your love for Him, your devotion and obedience to Christ. Your religious practice must be founded in hearing and doing God's Word (Matthew 7:24-27). Don't let your emotions guide you. Let God guide you through His Word. Don't let your emotions take over when you know what is right in the sight of

God. There is a false emotionalism in the religious world that may look good and seem attractive, but it is not the pure and undefiled religion of Christ you learn from the New Testament.

We should never confuse emotion with divine authority. You may hear someone say, *"I feel like God is leading me to…"* When someone says that, I want to ask them, "what has God already said in His Word?" Sometimes there is a temptation to listen to your feelings rather than read and study God's Word. God communicates to us through His Word. "…He has spoken to us by His Son," and His Son sent the Holy Spirit to guide the writers of the New Testament (see John 16:13; Eph 3:1-3; Jude 3). Something may feel right, but emotions can deceive us. The word of God will never deceive you. The danger is taking what you feel as truth rather than reading the truth God has revealed. "Our emotions and our appetites are good things. They can serve us well and contribute to the quality of our lives. But these things don't serve us well unless they've been trained to do so. Much that is good about life in this world depends upon freedom, and there is no freer person than the one who has learned how to use the word 'no.'" (*Enthusiastic Ideas*, by Gary Henry).

There are good emotions that lead to and accompany good behavior. Loving God is a good emotion that leads to obedience and ought to be present the rest of your life. Fearing God and keeping His commandments involves positive emotions. Just remember, all emotions must be governed by your knowledge of God's Word. (See Matt 22:37; Eccl 12:13,14; Prov 1:7). Please read the other chapters in this book. Love, control, respect, learning, forgiving, growing and developing are all within your reach if obedience to God's Word is your commitment. In each case there is an emotional component that is governed by Christ's example and teaching.

Shame can become a good emotion! At first it may seem strange to think of shame as a good emotion. But God gave us a mental capacity called "conscience." When the conscience is programmed with God's Word, and we violate His Word, we feel shame or guilt. That can be good **IF** it prompts genuine repentance. Never be ashamed to be a Christian (1 Pet. 4:15,16; Rom. 1:16; Luke 9:26). But when you violate God's Word, a legitimate emotion of guilt or shame can take us to repentance (Rom 6:21; 2 Cor 7:10).

Talking with someone you trust can be a good way to manage and express your emotions. It can be harmful to disguise hurt feelings and discouragement. Identify people you trust and seek their wise counsel. God's people who are diligent and mature are "filled with all knowledge" and "able to instruct," (Rom 15:14).

I wish for all of you who read this, that the gospel of Jesus Christ will be received by you through the activity of your faith. And, that you will rejoice that you can know Jesus Christ and go to heaven. "Do not be slothful in zeal, be fervent in spirit, serve the Lord," (Rom 12:11). You will not learn good emotional management from movies, Snapchat, Facebook or video games. You may not learn emotional management from your classmates at school. There may be adults in your life who do not illustrate good emotional maturity. You can learn this from the example and teaching of Jesus Christ.

From your Pawpaw

Questions

1. Why do we have emotions?

2. Why did God tell Cain "to rule over" his sin?

3. Why is knowledge of the life of Christ valuable for us on this subject?

4. Why do we sometimes need to slow down and count to ten?

5. Why is shame sometimes a good emotion?

12. Respect Mom and Dad

Bill Robinson

To My Grandsons.

Have you ever gotten separated from your mom and dad? Maybe you were in a big store somewhere, walking along with your mom, when you stopped to look at some toy that caught your eye. When you looked up, your mom was nowhere to be seen! Jesus got separated one time from his parents, a story told to us in the Scripture.

> Now his parents went to Jerusalem every year at the Feast of the Passover. And when he was twelve years old, they went up according to custom. And when the feast was ended, as they were returning, the boy Jesus stayed behind in Jerusalem. His parents did not know it, but supposing him to be in the group they went a day's journey, but then they began to search for him among their relatives and acquaintances, and when they did not find him, they returned to Jerusalem, searching for him. After three days, they found him in the temple, sitting among the teachers, listening to them and asking them questions. And all who heard him were amazed at his understanding and his answers. And when his parents saw him, they were astonished. And his mother said to him, "Son, why have you treated us so? Behold, your father and I have been searching

for you in great distress." And he said to them, "Why were you looking for me? Did you not know that I must be in my Father's house?" And they did not understand the saying that he spoke to them. And he went down with them and came to Nazareth and was submissive to them. And his mother treasured up all these things in her heart. And Jesus increased in wisdom and in stature and in favor with God and man. (Luke 2:41-52)

There are many wonderful lessons we can learn from this story. One of the great lessons we learn is what it means to respect mom and dad. Do you respect your mom and dad? Do you know what it means to respect someone? To respect someone is to show them that you care about and are truly interested in them. It is impossible to honor mom and dad without respecting them. In other words, to honor your father and mother is to respect them.

Can you imagine being separated from your mom and dad for three days, not knowing where they are? What if they also did not know where you were? What kind of mood would your mom be in if this happened to her? Do you think she would be afraid? Would she cry and be upset? What about you? Would you be scared and angry? You see, when all of these feelings are going through our minds and hearts, we have to be really careful of what we say and do next. If we speak quickly, without thought, it could lead us to say or do something disrespectful. Yet, in this story about Jesus getting separated from his parents, it is clear that Jesus understood some things that even his parents did not understand. Sometimes that happens. When his parents finally found him, his mother said, "Why have you worried us so?" Of course, that was never Jesus' intention. Nonetheless, even though Jesus' parents didn't necessarily understand the significance of what he was doing, Jesus did not argue with his parents. Instead, he shows them great respect. Respecting your parents does not mean they have to understand you. You honor your parents simple because they are your parents.

If I say to you, "Don't take your cue from the world," do you understand what I am saying? I am saying just because someone in the world (including someone on television), or one of your friends, acts in a way that is NOT showing respect for their mom and/or dad, or anyone else for that matter, don't follow their example. It is never acceptable for you to be disrespectful, no matter who else has been disrespectful to you, your parents, their parents, or anyone else. Even if someone mistreats you because they don't understand you or agree with you, you are not to act like them! Jesus makes this very point when He said, "So whatever you wish that others would do to you, do also to them, for this is the Law and the Prophets." (Matthew 7:12). We must take our cue from Jesus and show respect for mom and dad because that's the way we want to be treated, whether they understand or not.

We are reminded in the story that even though his parents did not completely understand him, "he went down with them and came to Nazareth and was submissive to them." He respected his parents so much that he didn't have to have his own way! The reason we know Jesus respected his parents is because the writer tells us he was submissive to them. Do you know what it means that he went down with them and was submissive? He went with them, even though he wanted to learn from the elders at the Jerusalem church, because he understood that he was still a child, and his parents were in charge of him. To be respectful, he had to do what they told him to do— that is what it means to be submissive. What we learn from Jesus is that our feelings are not as important as honoring or showing respect for our parents.

Another lesson about respect for mom and dad that we learn from this story is that your own self-respect (that is your respect for yourself) does not come from the feelings you have about yourself but rather from being the kind of person God wants you to be. I know you want to be the kind of person God wants you to be. To become that person, you must respect your mom and dad. Jesus truly respected himself as a young man because he respected his parents and he wanted to be the kind of person God wanted him to be; to respect yourself, you must expect godliness of yourself. "And Jesus increased in wisdom and in stature and in favor with God and man" (Luke 2:52).

Honoring your parents and showing them respect is truly the basis for honoring God! There is no proper honor due to our parents that EVER detracts from the honor and glory due to God! Let me emphasize this point by saying it this way as well. There is absolutely no honor or glory due to God that will ever take away from the proper honor that is due mom and dad! To the contrary, if the order of the 10 commandments means anything, then God places honoring father and mother—the fifth command—above the command not to murder, which is the sixth command. However, that is not surprising if we stop and think about the fact that what we said about respect for God goes hand in hand with honoring our parents. So, if we respect our parents, we will learn to respect God and we will honor life!

Honoring our parents is the very foundation of a CIVIL society. How sad that we live in a world which blatantly disrespects the sanctity of the home and dishonors parents. The failure to respect parents is seen on every hand in many nations around the world (including the United States of America). Where God is dishonored, blasphemed, and mocked with such cold indifference, violence becomes the rule, rather than the exception. We are not left without warning from God of what happens in a world where people are disobedient to their parents: "But understand this, that in the last days there will come times of difficulty. For people will be lovers of self, lovers of money, proud, arrogant, abusive, **disobedient to their parents**, ungrateful, unholy, heartless, unappeasable, slanderous, without self-control, brutal, not loving good, having the appearance of godliness, but denying its power. Avoid such people." (2 Timothy 3:1-5) Look at this list. Do you realize what is at the heart of it? At the very center of the list is "disobedient to their parents." A child who is not raised to respect and honor his parents is at the heart of much of our trouble in the home, school, and society. No wonder we are told to avoid such people!

We are also reminded of the importance of honoring parents in the New Testament (Eph 6:1-3; Col 3:20). Look again at how the apostle Paul spells respect and honor for mom and dad in these passages. "Children OBEY your parents in everything [in the Lord], for this pleases the Lord." In the Lord does not mean you must obey your parents only if they are Christians. The command is to you, not to them. Respecting/honoring your parents "in the Lord" is not about your parents' relation to the Lord, it is about your relation to the Lord—to be the kind of person the Lord wants you to be! Remember what we learned earlier in the story about Jesus getting separated from his family: He grew in favor with God as he was subject to his parents.

You respect your parents not only because they gave you your life but because they sustained your life, providing what you needed—food, shelter, and clothing when you could not provide for yourself! Respect for your parents continues as long as they live. As they advance in age they may become unable to take care of themselves and/or provide for themselves. You may have to care for them as they once cared for you, as a part of honoring and respecting them.

Look at the chapters in this book. I can assure you that without respect for mom and dad, your ability to learn will be greatly diminished, your love for God, neighbor or enemies will be nonexistent, you certainly will not be true to the Word, you won't be different from the world, you will not be firm in the faith, much less content, and you will not care about growing, forgiving, or controlling your emotions! Any evidence of such things in the life of one who does not respect/honor his parents is bound to be limited and an exception rather than the rule.

You are blessed to have parents who love the Lord, each other and you. They love you very much and that means they sometimes have to discipline you because they are trying to be the best parents they can possibly be. They realize that there is no success that can compensate for failure in the home. Unfortunately, not all of your friends may have moms and dads that love them and treat them like your parents do. In fact, the sad truth is, some parents can say and do mean things, and are unkind to their children. God does not like that at all! In Matthew 19:14, Jesus invites children to spend time with him, because he loved them. In Colossians 3:21, the Bible says that fathers shouldn't be mean to their children. But God expects all of us to be respectful of our parents even when they are not nice people. We always should do what God says first, and not do bad things even if our parents tell us to. But God still wants us to be kind to our parents, to not be rude or disobedient or disrespectful to them. That can be very hard for children who do not have nice parents! But it is what God expects. We can be good people even when other people in our families are not. You can help make a difference in the lives of other people by treating your mom and dad with respect!

I want to leave you with one last thought. If we go back to the story we read in Luke 2:41-52, verse 51-52, "And he went down with them and came to Nazareth and was submissive to them. And his mother treasured up all these things in her heart. And Jesus increased in wisdom and in stature and in favor with God and man." Jesus, by being submissive to his mom and dad as we discussed it, was a blessing to his mother's heart. In the very memory of her son, her heart treasured the time she had with him because he honored her and his father. Furthermore, as we have pointed out not only did Jesus do what he did in honoring his mom and dad to become the kind of person God wanted him to be, but he grew in stature and favor with God AND MAN! I want to emphasize that last one: AND MAN! Honoring and respecting mom and dad caused him to grow in favor with man. I cannot stress enough to you the importance of being respected for righteous qualities and in the same vein there is absolutely nothing wrong with being liked for righteous qualities. Respect for mom and dad is indeed a righteous quality that lays the groundwork for a solid foundation of a righteous life that will bring much honor and glory to God and to all who know you.

I love you Noah, CJ, Seth and Easton. Indeed, my heart is overflowing with the many treasures each one of you have placed there from every moment we spend together. I am so thankful and blessed to be your Grampy! Thanks for being my grandsons!

Love, Grampy

Questions

1. Why was Jesus submissive to his parents?

2. Why is honoring your mom and dad a righteous quality?

3. Why should we stop and think before we speak or act, if mom or dad have said something we disagree with or hurt our feelings?

4. Why is it important to understand the phrase "in the Lord" (Ephesians 6:1) to refer to children and not the parents?

5. Why is showing respect for mom and dad so important?

13. Develop Your Mind for God

Doy Moyer

To my dear grandchildren,

When your Marmee and I had our children, which includes one of your parents, I prayed often, asking God that they have "minds to do Your will." I wanted my children to learn to think better than I have, to be better servants of the Lord than I have been. I now continue to say that same prayer for you, my children's children, fervently praying to God on your behalf so that you will use your minds to do God's will. You can, and there is no better way to use your minds than to focus on God.

I want you to understand just how important your mind is. We may go through our day thinking, but are we thinking much about how to improve the minds? Please think about this with me for a few minutes. Let me also encourage you, if you have not done so, to read the other letters in this book. All of these men feel toward their grandchildren as I feel toward you. We all want what is best for you, and we desire so much to see you succeed in serving the Lord.

First, God has given you a mind.

What is your mind? Your mind is what you think with, decide with, and even feel with. It is not just the physical stuff inside your head; it is not mere material. It is the center of how you process information, how you form your attitudes, how you communicate with others, and how you decide the most important matters of life. In the Bible, sometimes the mind is even referred to as the heart, which includes the inner part of your thinking, your will, your desires, and your intentions. For example, Paul gives thanks for the Roman Christians because they obeyed "from the heart" what God desired (Rom 6:17). To do anything "from the heart" requires that it be in your mind, that you have thought it through, and that you really want to do it.

Your mind is a vital part of what makes you who you are as a human being made in God's image (Gen 1:26-27). Because God has given you your mind, you ought to learn to use it to think well and to bring glory to God. If you think of your mind as a gift from God, then you can also think about the fact that you need to treat that gift with respect. You can do this by thinking properly about God and what matters to Him. Your faith can grow as you pay attention to the mind of God revealed in the Scriptures by the Holy Spirit (Rom 10:17; 1 Cor 2:10-13). When we don't treat our minds properly, we will end up like those whose minds become "futile" or worthless because they let their minds dwell on things that are sinful and meaningless (Rom 1:21; Eph 4:17). Don't waste your mind; it is a beautiful gift of God to nurture. Make it better by serving God rather than wasting it on a world that cannot last.

Second, your mind is your responsibility.

God has given you your mind, and that means it is yours to take care of. Your thoughts are yours and no one else's. They are yours to control, yours to change, and yours by which you will make the most important choices you can ever make in your life. This is why it matters what you allow to go into your mind and what you think about most of the time. What you put into your mind will change who you are and how you behave in life. You will become a better person or a person who is angry, bitter, or even worse.

Because your mind is your own, be careful about how you listen to others. Jesus taught, "No one after lighting a lamp covers it with a jar or puts it under a bed, but puts it on a stand, so that those who enter may see the light. For nothing is hidden that will not be made manifest, nor is anything secret that will not be known and come to light. *Take care then how you hear*, for to the one who has, more will be given, and from the one who has not, even what he thinks that he has will be taken away" (Luke 8:16-18, ESV).

The way you listen to others and what you allow to come into your mind is a very important responsibility, but that is *your* responsibility. Be careful because once you give up your mind to the wrong things, you will be changed in ways you will regret.

Third, your mind is meant to be used well.

God wants you think thoughts that are worthy of praise. We all are to think about things that true, honorable, just, pure, lovely, commendable, excellent, and worthy of praise (Phil 4:8). The fruit of the Holy Spirit is "love, joy, peace, patience, kindness, goodness, faithfulness, 23 gentleness, self-control" (Gal 5:22). "Set your mind on the things above, not on the things that are on earth. For you have died and your life is hidden with Christ in God" (Col 3:2-3, NASU). By thinking "on things above," that is, on the things of the Spirit (Rom 8:6), you will be thinking about the most honorable and greatest matters possible. We can keep seeking what is above, where Christ is (Col 3:1). To get the most out of your mind, you will need to be thinking of God and what matters to Him all of your life. You will never waste time when you are focusing on Him.

However, your mind can also be used to think bad thoughts. The wise man said,

> Be not envious of evil men,
> nor desire to be with them,
> for their hearts devise violence,
> and their lips talk of trouble. (Prov 24:1-2)

The Bible warns about this problem over and over. This is why we all need to be so careful about what we allow into our minds, and what we spend time thinking about. We are to guard our hearts with all diligence because from our hearts come the most important matters of life (Prov 4:23). Jesus taught that from our hearts come bad thoughts, and those evil thoughts may well be turned into evil actions (Matt 15:19-20). If we do not watch what we think about and make sure we are submitting our thoughts to God, we may do things that we will later regret.

Fourth, you are in a battle for your mind.

There are forces out there trying influence you to think in ways that will hurt you. The devil is like a roaring lion seeking to devour, and we need to resist him (1 Pet 5:8). The apostle Paul wrote, "we do not wrestle against flesh and blood, but against the rulers, against the authorities, against the cosmic powers over this present darkness, against the spiritual forces of evil in the heavenly places" (Eph 6:12). This is why it is so important to stand firm in the Lord and put on His armor (read Ephesians 6:10-18). We have to prepare our minds to fight against all that would have us turn away from Jesus and His truth.

Paul was concerned about the Corinthians for the same reason. He feared that people were deceiving them and that their thoughts would be "led astray from a sincere and pure devotion to Christ" (2 Cor 11:3). If they didn't pay attention and guard their minds, they would be lost to the errors that would destroy their souls. This is always a concern, and it is so important that you be aware that this can happen if you don't watch what you allow to take root in your mind.

The apostle Peter has given us a great way to think about serving God. He wrote to Christians who were facing suffering and persecution, and he told them that they had been born again to a living hope through the resurrection of Jesus. They could look forward to the inheritance reserved in heaven, and they could be joyful even though their faith was tested. In the end, we have a great salvation awaiting (1 Pet 1:3-12). Because of what God has done for us, Peter wrote that we need *prepare our minds* for action so that we will be obedient children of God, learning to be holy in a world that is antagonistic (vv. 13-16; 1 Pet 4). Our thoughts, then, need to be brought under control to our Lord who gave Himself up for us.

Fifth, you are to love God with all your mind.

The greatest command is to love God, and one of the elements of that command is to love God with all your mind (Matt 22:37). All of the energy that we expend in how we think, what we think about, and how we use our thoughts ought to be directed toward loving and serving God.

This includes your intellectual abilities. As we grow, we learn, and we develop our minds so that we can think better, be wiser, and know more. All of that, in turn, helps us make the kinds of choices that please God. Remember, how we think impacts how we act. Loving God with all your mind means that you are always wanting to please Him. You are thinking about ways to serve Him and glorify Him.

You may be overwhelmed by a world that pushes you to educate yourself in many ways. Education is good when it is used in a godly, wise way. Yet of all that you do in education, the most important use of your mind will be in how to use it to serve God and others. No education is so important that it overshadows your need to be a Christian in service to the God who made you.

God does not want you to be ignorant and unthinking. As many have said it, God doesn't want you to "check your brains at the door" when you become a Christian. In fact, the most we will get from our minds will come when we see that our minds are the product of a thinking, intelligent Creator who made us this way. We can return this love by using our minds to serve Him.

How Can We Train Our Minds to Focus on God?

1. Keep first things first. Priorities are always important, but I am speaking here about what the apostle Paul says is "most important." This is the gospel message that Jesus Christ died for our sins, was buried, raised again on the third day, and appeared to many (1 Cor 15:1-4). When we keep this perspective on the grace of God, we can keep our focus on Jesus and know that everything we do for Him is worthwhile (v. 58). Never lose sight of this.

2. Read your Bible continually. The Holy Spirit has revealed God's mind so that we may understand what He wants (1 Cor 2:10-13). Faith comes by hearing God's word (Rom 10:17), so we want to make sure that we are reading, hearing, and studying the word continually. The message of God gives us hope, and this is our anchor in a world that wants us to take our minds off of God. Remember: "Man shall not live by bread alone, but by every word that comes from the mouth of God" (Matt 4:4). Then remember that Jesus is the only One to whom we may turn for our eternal salvation. "Lord, to whom shall we go? You have the words of eternal life" (John 6:68).

3. Pray often and regularly (1 Thess 5:17). When we are praying, we are especially focusing our minds on God. We are communicating with Him, telling Him what is on our minds and in our hearts. By praying regularly and often, we will be thinking in ways that will bring us closer to God. Prayer is such a vital part of our relationship with God. Never neglect it. We need to communicate with Him.

4. Talk with others about God. Engage in spiritual conversations with people. It is important to talk with non-Christians about Jesus, but I'm thinking even more about talking with other Christians about Jesus and the Scriptures. Ask questions with your Bible open. Go to your parents and talk with them about God. They will love that. Talk with older Christians who can share with you some insights and wisdom. Be open about your faith. And please, always, feel free to come talk with your Papa and Marmee about God or anything on your mind. We will cherish every minute with you, especially as we talk about the most important matters of life.

5. Constantly think about God, about Jesus, and the great teachings of the Bible. When you cannot talk with others, keep thinking about God. Think about Jesus and His teachings. Meditate on the great teachings of the Bible, mulling them over in your mind and trying to understand the deeper ideas that are there. The Scriptures are so powerful, and there is so much there to think about, ideas to connect together, and applications to draw out. Don't let your Bible study and your thoughts about the Bible become stale and dull. The Bible has such deep connections, and it's like an interwoven tapestry that presents a beautiful picture to us. Dive in. Think deeply. Study hard.

6. Avoid getting too comfortable with the world. The apostle John warns against loving the world (1 John 2:15-17). All that is in the world will pass away. We need to see, by faith, that there is more than just this world. Paul wrote that he was able to look not at the things that are seen, but at the things that are not seen, "for the things which are seen are temporal, but the things which are not seen are eternal" (2 Cor 4:18). If we get too comfortable with the world, we will forget about the eternal, and that is never good.

This doesn't mean that we completely forget about this world. We do live in this world, and God has given us work to do and things that we can enjoy while we are here. We have responsibilities that we cannot ignore. Yet we need to be aware that this world is temporary, and we have a greater purpose than to live only for this world. As Paul reminded the Philippians, the Christian's true citizenship is in heaven (Phil 3:20). If we can keep this in front of us, we will be using our minds for the kingdom of God.

7. Develop good thinking and reasoning skills. Thinking can be hard work, and it can take practice to learn how to think properly and well. The writer of Hebrews said that mature people have trained their senses (their minds) to discern good and evil (Heb 5:12-14). Train hard. Train well. Practice good thinking skills. Learn how to think logically. Try to understand what good reasoning looks like. This is something that you will continue to grow in as you become more mature. God expects us to develop good thinking habits. I pray that you will be committed to doing this as you continue to age and grow in Christ.

8. Commit yourself to doing what is right. Remember the wise man who built his house on the rock and the foolish man who built his house on the sand (Matt 7:24-27)? The wise man is the one hears Jesus and does what He says. He is committed to doing what it right. The foolish man doesn't listen or try to do what is right. By committing ourselves to doing what is right, we are establishing a way of thinking for ourselves, a way that is not wishy-washy and uncertain (see Eph 4:14). It is a way that will look to God and seek His will above all else. It is a decision made in the mind, and this is exactly the kind of mind God wants.

By committing ourselves to doing what is right, we are committing ourselves to serving others. This follows what our Lord did (Mark 10:44-45). We are thereby learning not to do what we do because of envy, hatred, or arrogance. It is a path to humility, love, and seeking to put others first. It is following the mind of Christ (Phil 2:3-5).

As my grandchildren, I feel a special bond with you. I also know I have a great responsibility. I often pray for you as Paul prayed for the Colossians: "And so, from the day we heard, we have not ceased to pray for you, asking that you may be filled with the knowledge of his will in all spiritual wisdom and understanding, so as to walk in a manner worthy of the Lord, fully pleasing to him, bearing fruit in every good work and increasing in the knowledge of God" (Col 1:9-10).

Marmee and I always expected our children to serve God. We never considered failing in this to be an option. We expect the same from you, and our expectations of who you are and what you can accomplish will always remain positive. Just remember that God—the Father, Son, and Holy Spirit—is always there to help. Jesus will help you in temptations (Heb 2:18; 4:15-16). Your parents will help you. Your brothers and sisters in Christ will help you. We will help you. We are always here for you.

I love you so much more than I am able to say, and all that I want for you may be summed up in this: love God with all your heart, soul, strength, and mind, and love your neighbors as yourself. Use your minds to bring glory to God.

With all my love for Joshua, Elizabeth, Abigail, Eliana, Nathan …

Papa

Questions

1. Why is it important to think of your mind as a gift from God?

2. Why should you be careful about how you listen to others?

3. Why should we be focusing on what is "worthy of praise"?

4. How is there a battle for the mind? What does this mean?

5. How can we learn to love God with all our mind?

6. Why do we need to work so hard at good thinking?

7. Discuss the seven suggestions. Can you think of any more?

Made in the USA
Columbia, SC
06 July 2025